Phyllis
SARGENT
An English Memoir

Mary (9), Phyllis (7), Bobby (4)

Phyllis SARGENT

An English Memoir

EDITED BY

LOUISE WILSON

WHITE CACTUS
IPSWICH SUFFOLK

PHYLLIS SARGENT
An English Memoir

First published in 2007 by
WHITE CACTUS
PO Box 660, Ipswich, Suffolk IP1 9AH
E-Mail: louise@white-cactus.com

ISBN 978-0-9556065-0-2

Produced and printed by members of
THE GUILD OF MASTER CRAFTSMEN

Cover, Book Design and Typesetting by Cecil Smith
Typeset in Minion

Printed and bound in Great Britain by
RPM PRINT & DESIGN
2-3 Spur Road, Quarry Lane, Chichester, West Sussex PO19 8PR

Contents

Fr. Dermot Fenlon

Acknowledgement

gratefully acknowledge the assistance of Father Dermot Fenlon whose unstinting help made this book possible. Father Dermot has been a great friend to Phyllis Sargent for many years and was instrumental in her conversion to Catholicism. He helped me to pull this project together by offering insights into theological points and historical facts about Phyllis's life. He waded through several versions of this book and helped bring it to life.

Louise Wilson

Aug 2006, Phyllis with Louise and Katie Wilson

Introduction

I am fascinated by Phyllis Sargent's life story as to me it is so very inspiring both in terms of her deep faith, close friendships and is symbolic of a very specific time in English history.

My mother, Jill Carsen, was a close friend of Phyllis for over thirty years and she often went to have afternoon tea with her. When I am with Phyllis a feeling of such peace envelops me. All the worries of this disposable modern age disappear in her presence. No matter what health issues of her own that she is enduring she is always concerned with helping other people.

Phyllis has left an amazing legacy, from the people whose lives she has touched, to the people who will be affected by reading her story. This is despite her self deprecating words in the opening chapter 'I do not feel fulfilled as a woman, particularly as I have no children or grandchildren to live on as part of me'.

Louise Wilson,
August 2006

Phyllis with Zulu baby

An Anglican Life

I have less than five years to go before I reach my allotted span of life, my three score years and ten, so unless I am given bonus time, my span is nearly up. As I look back on my life, which has not been eventful or exciting and as I have not married, I do not feel fulfilled as a woman, particularly as I have no children or grandchildren to live on as part of me. All I can do is to leave a scratchy sketch of my life, but for whom? There is no one to read it who would find it at all interesting.

As I reflect over my life I can trace my development as a Christian though I would have to live many more years than I will be given to attain anything like the person I was intended to become. All through my life I can trace people who have been stepping stones to lead me onwards towards my goal. I had a very good start in life with good Christian parents, who had a simplicity in their religion and a way of life which was moral and good and here I was most fortunate. I was for many years what one would call a 'middle of the road' churchwoman, first going to Matins and Evensong on Sundays and then progressing to a weekly Parish

Phyllis' text from now on, to the header '1985 to 1987 Phyllis' Reception into the Catholic Church' was composed between 1977 and 1984.

Communion. I cannot say that I understood my religion at all. It was simply something one did on Sundays. My parents went to church and I was expected to go with them – it was as simple as that – we did not demur about going but treated it as the norm and part of life.

So the church has been the centre of my life from the very beginning and before it, for my parents were married in the church where later, I was Baptised and Confirmed and later still both my parents were buried from the same church. So, as I write, it is obvious that we come from God without anything and return to God at the end of our lives leaving all our worldly possessions behind us.

All we take with us is our inner selves, our personality and what we have made of the life God has given us. Looking back on my life there is much one wishes had been left unsaid and undone and much one wishes had been done but was omitted. We can only start each day from where we are and I realise now that possessions do not matter. The only thing that matters is how much we have loved, how much we have cared about others and accepted the life which has been given to us.

It is not about fighting circumstances and continually thinking 'if only' because this is the life that God has entrusted to me with all its situations and it is up to me to thank God for it and to live each day as if my last. I am of course very conscious that I do not do this at all well and I have all the proneness to sin as has everyone else for I know what it is to feel depressed for no apparent reason, to feel jealousies and resentments. However, by being very conscious of these hazards I can offer them up to God and try even to thank Him for them. This is because it is in our own personal circumstances and limitations that we can grow and it is when we are striving against odds and disappointments that the growth is sometimes more rapid. I thank God for the great opportunities which have been given to me and the wonderful people I have met in the course of my life.

Mother

Mary, Mother, Granny, Great Granny

Daddy, Mother, Mary, Phyllis

1924, Bobby Age 4

Phyllis, Bobby, Mary

Mary and Bobby, Halsted, Essex

Phyllis, Pat and other Girl Guides

1940, Mother, Bobby, Father,
Mary and Dogs

A Young Miles

*"While the singing was going on, my sister,
brother and I would creep out of our beds and sit
on the stairs to listen to the adults below and
then often go downstairs to the dining room and
eat up the remains of the meal."*

I was born in Halstead, Essex on 6th February 1917, towards the end of the First World War and the year of the Russian Revolution – the quiet age of the horse and cart for there were only a few cars when I was born. My childhood memories are happy ones. I was surrounded by love and lived a care-free existence. My methods of travelling were on bicycle, by bus or occasionally by train. My father was in his fifties when I was born and I loved him dearly. I can still remember his kind blue eyes and white hair and immaculate dress with his always carefully creased trousers. I remember his hands and his snake ring with small diamonds for its eyes, which I now treasure. I recall holding his hand and remembering how my arm ached when I was little because I had to hold it up so high. How he took my sister and me to the draper's shop and bought us ribbon for our hair. He was very musical, sociable, full of fun and very polite.

I remember my mother who was about twenty five years younger than my father and looking back I think she was one of the best Christian women I have ever met. She was quite selfless and would find it hard to tell an untruth. All she asked of life was that her family was happy. She asked nothing for herself and she stands out in my life as one of the purest women I have known. She was of average height with black hair and fresh complexion and the bluest eyes I have ever seen. She usually wore blue to complement her eyes. She used no make-up and this was typical of her – she was completely natural.

She loved cats especially and had a special cat language of her own when talking to her cat. She loved her family and I can recall now her devotion if one of us was ill. I can see the fire we would have in our bedroom and the flames reflected in patterns on the ceiling from the nursery fireguard. I felt so protected and secure in her presence and if something went wrong it was heaven to come home and tell her about it. For then it always seemed better or not so bad if my mother knew what the trouble was. She was a deeply religious woman, though not ostentatious about it. She had a deep faith and often I would catch glimpses of her on her knees praying as I passed her half open door. She had a great sense of humour and often when she laughed, her laughter was mixed with tears.

Most of our provisions were delivered to the house. The fishmonger, the grocer, and the bread-man used to come in his horse and cart and so did the milkman who was the son of a nearby farmer. The milk was brought in churns and we put out jugs to be filled. There must have been many germs about but we never seemed to be any the worse for that. There were always policemen on point duty and a water cart would come round periodically and water the roads – to lay the dust I suppose. Many buses were open-air doubled decked and we used to sit on top exposed to the elements and we would put out our hands to catch branches of trees as we went along.

There were a few motor cars but we did not possess one. However, my grandmother bought a car and she also employed a man to look after it and drive her about. She wore a motoring veil tied under her chin.

We often saw the 'fever van' and I remember being filled with a kind of awe as people were taken to the isolation hospital. Also when people were ill, sawdust used to be put down outside their homes to lessen the noise of the traffic as it passed. In the Spring, children used to bowl their hoops and spin their tops and play hopscotch on the pavements. Children were not as sophisticated as they are today and made their own amusements.

My parents' life together was happy in spite of the differences in age, and in consequence we children, my sister and my brother and I had a very happy and protected life. I remember being very shocked when I heard someone telling a lie because until the age of about twelve I had not met it and thought everyone spoke the truth.

My parents used to give bridge parties. After supper my father would play the piano and one of the guests would sing a solo and the rest join in the chorus. I can still recall these parties and I remember hearing my mother's laughter above all the rest. I must add that she was a very shy person but a wonderful hostess in her own home where she felt secure. While the singing was going on, my sister, brother and I would creep out of our beds and sit on the stairs to listen to the adults below and then often go downstairs to the dining room and eat up the remains of the meal.

My young life was a simple and sheltered one. I had a governess who taught me to read and write and do sums until I was six and then I went to the preparatory school, part of the Grammar school and then later into the big school itself. I liked school and made friends easily. I loved all games and was good at most of them. I was on the hockey field whenever possible in winter and on the tennis courts in summer. I also spent a lot of time swimming. I can recall the pleasure of going to the local swimming pool with my friends and eating currant buns afterwards which cost ½d each.

At the age of eleven, I met a girl called Pat who had recently come into the town. Her father was Manager of Westminster Bank and she lived in a large house with an equally large garden where we used to play. In summer we spent a lot of time climbing trees. In the garden there was a mulberry tree and we used to put on our swimsuits and sit up the tree eating the mulberries with all the stain of the mulberry juice falling on us.

Another great joy was to practice long jump for hours at a time on sand near the stables. Although I don't recall that either of us excelled in any way it was great fun. When staying at her home, before dressing, we used to spend hours in our pyjamas turning somersaults over the beds and landing on the floor the other side. These were highlights!

After hockey matches we would go to my home and eat hot jam tarts as soon as a batch came out of the oven. Our family was not well off and I always seemed to be wearing clothes belonging to my sister who was older than me or else from friends who had outgrown them. I was very conscious that I never really had the right clothes to wear and I think that is why I am so particular now about dress.

I also never had any pocket money so Pat always used to buy me sweets and ice creams for she had a generous allowance of 2/6d per week. We belonged to a company of Girl Guides and had wonderful camping holidays which I enjoyed tremendously. I remember feeling a little embarrassed when my parents met the train on our return as Pat's parents never did. I envied her the freedom she was given, but later on in life I learnt how she envied our united family. She told me she often felt unwanted. How little we understand of life when we are young.

Pat was an extrovert. She liked acting and I can see her now as a young school girl standing by my father's side as he played the piano singing the songs of the day. A particular favourite was 'tiptoe through the tulips'. I envied Pat's courage and freedom to sing like this. Later on she used to act in the local Dramatic Society and took the young leads and was very good. I was much too shy to do anything like this but used to sell programmes instead.

From the age of about twelve, I played golf. My father was very keen and so my sister, brother and I owned a few cut down clubs and learned to play. At that age one acquires a natural swing and my brother's was particularly good and he and I used to play together in competitions. Because we spent so much time on the golf course we went away with a lot of the prizes. I remember I won the Ladies Captain prize most years. I think if I had taken up golf seriously I might have done quite well at it. I played for the Club in matches and later on was the Captain of the Ladies side of the club. I used to play in foursomes with my Father and friends of his. I always carried my father's clubs as well as my own and would find his lost balls for him.

We had a very pleasant garden and I always seemed to be shearing banks or pulling the lawn mower with Daddy steering it. I was not allowed to go off and play tennis until I had done my bit of gardening. We all played croquet and often we played a foursome. However, Daddy would get so cross because we used to croquet him and send his ball off to the far end of the garden just as he was in a good position to get it through his hoop! My mother was excellent at croquet, as she was at all games and could hit a ball through a hoop at almost any angle.

I recall tea in the garden and looking back over the years the summers seemed to be always hot and I can even now hear the chink of cups and hear the wasps buzzing round the strawberry jam. These were happy carefree days living in the midst of love and knowing we were loved. How fortunate we were. I remember once thinking I was clever and told a rather rude joke to friends of my parents. I asked 'Why can't an engine sit down?' and then proceeded to tell them 'because it has a tender behind'. My parents were not amused!

As a family we always went to church and each Sunday morning our pew was filled up with the five of us. I would sit next to my father and hold his hand during the sermon. In my teens I taught in Sunday School, though I never went to Sunday School myself. It was here that I met a Missionary from South Africa who was Matron of a leper hospital. She made a great impression on me at the time and may have influenced my life later in some way. I suppose we liked going to church for I remember one Good Friday, my father wanted me to make up a foursome for golf and I wanted to go to the three hour service at Church. My mother suggested I went at 12 o'clock for one and a half hours and then went to play golf. I remember her words to me, she said 'You will be doing far more good by going with daddy for you will not have him always'. I am glad even now that I played golf that afternoon with my father.

Soon after I left school the Second World War broke out which ended our carefree life. We came up against the horrors of war and the loss of life of our many friends. This made me realize that my father was old and often I would wake up in the morning crying because I dreamed that he had died. As a teenager I spent much time on the tennis courts and golf courses and my brother and I played a lot together. We were also fond of cycling and spent much time cycling round the villages with our friends. Every Good Friday, Bobby and I went off on our bicycles at about 7am in the morning and we cycled through the villages near our home singing *Ride on, ride on in Majesty* and eating large quantities of hot cross buns. We did this every year, in fact until the War years – then everything took on a different note. I remember one of the men in the office saying that war brought out the best and worst in people – this I found to be true.

The first real crisis in my life was when Bobby, my brother, volunteered for the Army although he was under age at the time of Munich (1938). I remember so well that Sunday morning of September 3rd, 1939 when we returned from Church and switched on our wireless sets and heard Mr Chamberlain saying that we were at war with Germany. A heaviness filled our hearts and also a sense of unreality. Gone were the carefree days of my youth.

I remember so well, my brother, whom I loved so much, in his battle dress and forage cap waving goodbye to us from his little Morris Minor car, which he had bought for £10. That was the first time I had seen my father cry and it upset me very much. My brother was cheerfully singing to us in his unmusical voice as he drove off. He was singing the Gracie Fields song *Wish me luck as you wave me goodbye, cheerio, here I go on my way.*

Soon after this, my sister volunteered for the VADs and worked in a military convalescent home for six months. She loved the work and was good at it, but alas her health broke down and she was forced to give it up. This chronic mastoid handicapped her from doing a job all her life. My mother persuaded me not to go into the forces as at that time my sister and brother were away in the forces. She said that daddy was no longer young.

Therefore I worked in a munitions factory which made aeroplane parts and Bailey Bridges etc. I worked in the office as I knew one of the Directors of the firm because I had stayed in his house when I was a child with his niece, Jean, who was a school friend. I kept up a correspondence with Jean along with my other school friend Pat for many years. On the whole I enjoyed myself at this factory and met a very mixed batch of people.

I had not come across men much before, at least not in the way they were at this place and I had a very rude awakening. They made advances to me and I thought they were merely being friendly and I encouraged them. It was not until later that I realised I had not behaved wisely. I blame my mother a little for this because I was not told much about the facts of life and if I had known more I would have behaved more prudently.

During the early War years my sister was serving away in a military hospital as a VAD and my brother was a gunner in the Essex Yeomanry but later transferred into the RAF as a fighter pilot in Coastal Command. I was very fond of my brother and he wrote to me 'from a ditch somewhere in England' and told me of his wish to go into the RAF before he told our parents. He quoted Colonel Lovelace's poem 'I could not love thee dear so much, loved I not honour more'.

Looking back I remember when he was confirmed at the age of about fourteen or fifteen. This made a deep impression on him. In the fly leaf of the little book of prayers given to him by his vicar, Canon Curling, was written the text the bishop had given at his Confirmation service address. It was 'Be thou faithful unto death and I will give thee a crown of life'. Bobby signed this underneath and wrote 'I will do my best'. He did.

He trained as a pilot in Canada and became an Officer in the RAF and was asked to stay behind to train others, but he refused saying that particular job was for a married man. It was his duty to be in the front line. In 1941, our cousin, Teddy, was killed as a result of a raid on Malta. He was a pilot in Bomber Command. Before, I thought 'young men will die', but it was not until Teddy was shot down over Malta, that I realised Bobby might die too.

One night, just before Bobby went back to camp after a short leave, he put his hands on my shoulders and said 'Phil, I will not be coming back'. I was horrified and protested and said 'of course you will', but he was quite calm and said 'no, I won't come back. The old man can take it but do take care of mother'. He was an idealist and hoped to become a Priest after the war but sadly a short time after he had said those words to me, he was shot down in the North Sea in November 1942, on the feast of St. Edmund.

My mother who had a sixth sense, asked us to send a pre-paid telegram to Bobby, for in a dream she had seen him in the water all night. The telegram came back in due course with the dreaded words 'We deeply regret to inform you, etc. etc.'. Mother was right. She had seen him in the water. The telegram continued 'Missing believed killed' but to this day we have never had confirmation of his death.

After this the fun seemed to go out of life. I still played tennis and golf and went to dances and became engaged to a young man who was a Captain in the 4th Indian Division. However, after the war when he returned, he had changed and we broke off the engagement.

We had a very dear friend, Louise Hughes, living alone, as her husband had died, and her children were away. She and my mother were great friends. Louise often came to our house in those war years. She used to sit with us in the cellar during raids. I always sat with my father and one night as we emerged from the cellar, Louise said 'listen to your father'. He was singing part of the hymn, *Abide with me – I fear no foe*. We kept in touch with Louise's daughters for many years. The son of one of them is Robert Fox who became a war correspondent on the Hermes in the South Atlantic recording messages about the Falkland crisis for the BBC.

During the war years there were tragedies all around us and we lost most members of our family. Granny died in 1940, Teddy was killed in 1941, Bobby in 1942, my sister's fiancé died in 1943, my father died in 1944 and my mother in 1945. A month before my mother died, my engagement was broken off.

Bobby in Uniform

Canada, Bobby far left

COASTAL COMMAND 'PLANES FLY IN TO ATTACK AN ENEMY CONVOY

Photographs of an attack made by aircraft of Coastal Command on a convoy of enemy supply ships off the Dutch coast. The large vessel in the centre of the convoy was later successfully torpedoed amidships. The lower picture shows bombs bursting around the ships.

Newspaper Article, Bobby's enemy convoy attack

Newspaper Article, Bobby Missing in Action

GERMAN CONVOY SMASHED

THREE SHIPS HIT

Two German supply ships and an escort vessel were hit on Friday in a daylight torpedo attack by Coastal Command aircraft on a heavily defended convoy near The Hague, states the Air Ministry.

Despite a tremendous barrage of gunfire from the ships and their escorts, followed by attacks by Focke-Wulf and Messerschmitt fighters, our aircraft swept in to the attack. One torpedo hit the main target—a big ship in the centre of the convoy—amidships. Soon afterwards a small supply ship was enveloped by a large explosion and began to list, and an armed trawler was left hidden in a cloud of steam and smoke.

Three of our aircraft are missing. A fourth, though hit by two cannon shells, one of which tore a big hole in the underside of the fuselage and smashed the hydraulic system, while the other passed clean through the fuselage and sheared off the port wing tip, got home and made a successful belly landing.

−6/11/42

1/L STEPHENSON, J,
Officers' Mess,
NORTH COTES
Lincs.

Dear Miss Sargent,

Pilot officer Noble has shown to me the letter which you wrote to him.

I'm afraid I can tell you little of any comfort to you in your anxiety.

1942, Letter from Bobby's Commander

"During the war years there were tragedies all around us and we lost most members of our family. Granny died in 1940, Teddy was killed in 1941, Bobby in 1942, my sister's fiancé died in 1943, my father died in 1944 and my mother in 1945. A month before my mother died, my engagement was broken off."

This meant that my sister and I were the only ones left out of a family of five. My sister remained at home and to make ends meet had paying guests. She was very friendly with one who stayed in the house and so I felt free to get a job in London, which I did at St Thomas's hospital. I will never forget leaving home that Sunday morning to settle into my expensive flat in Kensington, Beaufort Gardens near Harrods. I felt very bereft and that night I remember feeling that my parents and Bobby were very close to me and this was a great comfort. The flat proved to be too expensive and my cousin, May, who was then working for a doctor in Harley Street, got me into the club where she was living. St Clements house was close to Great Portman Street Tube Station and we called ourselves 'The Belles of St. Clements'.

It was during my time in London that I got to know my cousin well and we have been great friends ever since. We used to play golf with Dick and another friend of his and we spent many a happy day playing golf in the afternoon and evening and then going out to dinner. Staying in the Club were girls working in the big teaching hospitals in London and some worked at the BBC and the British Council, etc.

We were lucky in being offered free tickets for Radio shows like

Much Binding in the Marsh and *Itma*. We also went to musical concerts at the Albert Hall and I think I saw most plays of the day from the Gods (the cheap seats high up in the theatre). I saw plays such as *Oklahoma, Annie Get Your Gun, The Linden Tree* and *Bless the Bride*. Also we went to the Ballet and saw *Swan Lake* and *Die Fledermaus* at the Saddlers Wells theatre. We also played tennis in Regents Park.

This was all a great experience and I got to know certain parts of London very well. In the winter at the Club we played table tennis and I was pleased when I won the cup the year I was there. We played other Clubs too. We also went to Queens Park Skating Rink. I was never any good at skating but my cousin was very ambitious and a pretty good skater doing fancy steps while I clung to the edge and skated at an angle of 45 degrees. It was very pleasant skating to the tunes of the skaters waltz etc. and having refreshments during the evening and watching others on the rink.

My work at St. Thomas's hospital was on the whole dull but I made some good friends there. I had the opportunity of organizing the last of the Alexander Rose Day Appeal in 1948 for the Westminster area before the hospitals were nationalised. This was great fun. I remember feeling very important telephoning Downing Street and afterwards I was invited to the Mansion House where all organisers were given refreshments. It was quite an experience to go inside the Mansion House and later I was invited to Lambeth Town Hall to have coffee with Princess Marina who was President of the Alexander Rose Day Appeal.

It was when I was living in London that I made my first Retreat. I read about this when reading my Bible one evening from the B.R.F. notes. It intimated that anyone who was interested should write to Eccleston Square to the Secretary of the APR. I did this and fixed up to go to a weekend Retreat in Chiswick. I was a real novice and didn't really know anything about Retreats, but something happened to me while I was there which led me on to make regular Retreats.

It was a short time after this that I had another experience and I can remember it all so clearly, even to the exact place and time. I was on my way to St. Thomas's hospital and crossing over Westminster Bridge from the Houses of Parliament, when suddenly I was filled with a beautiful warm glow which I knew was God speaking to me and He had made it plain that He had a special job for me to do for Him. This may sound stupid to the reader but I can vouch that it is true. I told my sister when I went home for the next weekend, however, nothing happened for nearly a year. When it came, I knew that this was what I had been waiting for.

Some time after this, my sister was at home alone and she wanted me to return, so I got a job as secretary to the Principal of a technical college some seven miles away from my home. This job I enjoyed very much and here again I met some very interesting people on the staff. I corresponded with some of them for many years. The work was hard and varied. I had to deal with members of staff, students and parents, which was interesting. The staff used to laugh and congratulate me when I was taking letters from the Principal because he penned up a notice on the door of his room, 'Engaged' when I was with him, so as not to be disturbed!

It seems strange looking back on these working days that my means of transport was by bus or train, I did not own a car and only a very few of my friends did. Our boy friends had cars and that was sufficient for our needs.

While I was doing this job, a cousin came to stay with us, he was a priest and some twenty seven years older than me so I looked upon him more like an uncle. He had been in community jobs most of his life apart from being Vicar of St. Matthew's Church in Westminster. He had been Librarian at Pusey House, Oxford, and Chaplain of several Boys schools – St. Edward's School, Oxford and Marlborough College. At the time he visited us he was Chaplain of Woodard Kings College, Taunton.

Miles was in his late fifties and thought he ought to leave academia and live in a quieter atmosphere. After his stay with us it became evident to my sister and me that we should offer to make a home with Miles. We met with Miles' sister Margie (our cousin) and brother-in-law Frank, to discuss plans. Margie and Frank thought the idea an excellent one all round. I will not easily forget that visit to their home as I had eaten crab on the way there in the train and I think it must have been 'off' as I spent the night feeling very ill and sick! *

Frank was headmaster of Lancing College in Sussex, a Woodard School. They lived in a very large and beautiful house with a staff including a butler – all very grand. We did not know our cousins' daughters very well. They were a very clever family. The eldest, Ann, who was the same age as Bobby, married a one time head boy of Lancing, a stockbroker, and they had two small daughters. Mary, the second, read Classics and Philosophy at London University and was at the time working in the Foreign Office. She later became a nun at the community of the Holy Name, Malvern, and for many years spent her Rests with us. Elizabeth, the youngest daughter was

---

*For those who may not be familiar with Anglican worship, what follows is best understood as Phyllis' introduction to an aspect of Anglican tradition which had its roots in the 19th Century. The development of the Oxford Movement from the 1830s and 1840s ensured that a significant number of Anglicans sought to go behind the Anglican Reformation of the 16th Century to the Catholic tradition, and to recover for Anglicans a style of liturgical worship, including veneration of the Virgin Mary and a variety of ritual practices which had been alien to the Church of England until this time. The Woodard Schools were established to re-catholicise the Church of England. Among these, Lancing College held a place of pre-eminence. Those who taught and worshipped in such an environment used a language to refer to the Anglican worship as 'the Mass' and believed that there was no real difference between what they were reviving in the Church of England and what was the tradition of the Catholic Church. A notable contribution to this tradition of Anglicanism was made by the community of Mirfield. Father Raynes who features in the text, was Superior of the Community of the Resurrection at Mirfield while Phyllis's cousin, Miles, was at Pusey House, Oxford and it was from these Anglican clergy that Phyllis and Mary learned the Anglican understanding of the Catholic faith.

at Oxford University reading History. She later did probation work with children and went to Canada. In her thirties she followed her sister Mary into the Convent. Elizabeth has spent several years in Lesotho, South Africa, but on account of many operations on her feet was forced to come back to England where she became Guest Mistress at Malvern and was extremely good at it.

As a result of all this, in January 1950, Mary and I left our home in Essex and travelled to our new home in Wantage, Berkshire, where Miles had been appointed sub-warden of the Community of St. Mary the Virgin (Wantage). This is I believe the largest Anglican Order of Nuns in the world. We lived at White Lodge which was a beautiful house with a large garden, quite close to the Convent. We had in those days no central heating and we walked about the house in our top coats to keep warm. Miles' study was a large room with a barrel shaped ceiling and off the room was his bedroom. Mary slept on the same floor, but I went up another flight of stairs and had my bedroom and sitting room there from where I worked. Downstairs we had a large drawing room, dining room, kitchen and a chapel where Mass could be said and which we used quite a lot for our prayers.

I think Mary enjoyed being in Wantage better than I did. I found it very boring at first as I had no job to do and as I had been working since I was eighteen it felt very strange with nothing to do except housework, which I do not really enjoy. For another thing we did not understand the worship. We had not been used to High Masses, incense, Sanctus bells etc. and found it all rather strange. However, Miles was wonderful and we asked endless questions.

I remember taking my Prayer Book to one of the Services and the Chaplain's wife who was sitting next to me said 'I don't think you will find it in that dear'. Another time when I asked her about the Imposition of the Ashes on Ash Wednesday, she said 'if you have a sense of humour I advise you not to go'. I afterwards saw what she meant.

I remember feeling a real sense of worship sitting behind the screen with all the nuns in chapel and watching the incense rise and get caught up with the stream of sunlight pouring through the windows. I felt I knew what 'worship' was.

The Purification was the nuns' feast day and on 2nd February they had wonderful celebrations starting with a High Mass and I will never forget Bishop Furze coming down the chapel in his cope and mitre (he was at least 6 foot 5 inches in height) with the Asperges* and in those days everyone genuflected.

The singing of the nuns was an inspiration with the plainsong and all the alleluias. The nuns always bobbed when they met a Priest or Reverend Mother, so different from today when little or no reverence of this kind is made. So one day in the Chapel at the Convent it all fell into place and the Catholic worship and Faith is the most wonderful thing that has happened to me and we have to thank Wantage for this.

We had not been there very long before Mary had to have another operation on her ear. She had this in the Radcliffe Infirmary in Oxford but as a result of the operation her face was paralysed and it was a year or more before it became normal again. This was a very trying time for my sister for she wanted to hide when anyone came to the house because her mouth was twisted and she couldn't pronounce b's or p's. At night she had to close her eyes with her hands because the lids wouldn't function. Later on in the summer I remember visiting some cousins and when we went into a telephone kiosk to make a call, my sister looked into the mirror and saw her face begin to move. Thanks be to God, it soon became normal again after that.

During our time at Wantage, I took a part-time job and worked for a Mrs Turner in Sparsholt. She was a very talented woman. She was an Oxford Graduate, had a herd of Jersey cows, was Director of

---

* Note: the Asperges is, in the Latin liturgy, the sprinkling of the faithful with holy water.

a Coffee firm in Sussex, ran the village shop and post office and wrote for Punch! She was great fun. Her cousin, Arthur Pears, brother of Peter Pears the singer, helped her. Mrs Turner wrote a play for the villagers and produced it. She said that it was no trouble getting the villagers to act, for they just had to be themselves. She had written the play around them. It was a great success.

While we were at Wantage we met several celebrated people in the church. I will never forget my first meeting with Father Raymond Raynes, the then Superior of the Community of the Resurrection, Mirfield. Miles had known him at Oxford when he was at Pusey House and Father Raynes had been an Undergraduate.

Mary answered the doorbell one evening to Father Raynes and took him up to Miles' room. She came back into the drawing room where I was and said 'Phyl, I have just seen St. Peter!' Father Raynes was very tall, gaunt and thin. His head was shaven and his eyes were very blue and penetrating and set deep into his face. His nose was like a bird's beak and his voice and words abrupt and very much to the point. He wore a black cassock and belt with a crucifix hanging from it. Father Raynes was Superior of his Community and also Warden of the Convent which meant he visited the Convent several times a year and stayed for about a week at a time.

After he had been to our house once or twice Miles wanted us to meet him properly and so he used to come to the drawing room after that and soon we got to know him very well. In winter we had a roaring fire and Father Raynes drank endless cups of tea and talked and talked. We, Mary and I, sat on the floor at his feet and listened spellbound. These evenings were pure magic, we loved Miles and we loved Father Raynes and we learnt all about the Catholic faith and Africa. I afterwards asked Miles which dioceses Father Raynes was talking about and he said he thought it was Zanzibar but wasn't sure. I said thinking it funnier still, 'Are you sure it wasn't Zululand' and of course it was Zululand and Swaziland.

Later Father Raynes talked to me about a job and he said he would give me until the weekend to make up my mind. The job was organising secretary and treasurer for the diocese of Zululand and Swaziland working the whole of England. I would have to raise money, organise meetings at which I would speak, have money-raising functions over the country, keep the accounts and attend Council meetings in London and also arrange deputation tours for Bishops, priests and workers when they returned to England on furlough.

I afterwards said to Miles that I could not possibly do the job but he said that I could and most of all I knew this was the job God was asking me to do when I walked over Westminster bridge some years before.

I was told that a Priest's wife, a Mrs King, living in Holland Road, Notting Hill Gate London had done this job but could not do it justice as she had an ill husband at the time and a small son to look after as well as their home. I was free and had no ties, so I suppose was more fitted to do the job than she was so far as commitments were concerned.

I remember so well travelling to London by train to collect what files and things there were to start my office. I met Mrs King, who I liked immediately and until her death treasured her as one of my dearest friends. She said on seeing me 'Oh you are young, the Council members will love you'. Gillian King was most attractive, I suppose she was some 15 – 20 years older than me but we liked one another on sight and I was often a visitor in her house. When I had collected all the effects, maps, files, typewriter etc. and took them out to the waiting taxi, the taxi driver gave me one look and said 'Sure you 'aven't forgotten the piana, Miss'. Miles met me at Challow Road Station and motored me back to Wantage.

Eric Trapp had been asked by the Archbishop of Cape Town, Archbishop Clayton, if he would be Bishop of Zululand and Swaziland. He went on to say the diocese was dying and would he become Bishop in order to bury it. I may add that Eric Trapp was made Bishop at the age of 36 and now I believe holds the record for the longest living Bishop in the Anglican Communion. When Eric was asked by the Archbishop of Cape Town, if he would consider becoming Bishop of Zululand he was then on furlough in England from a missionary job in Basutoland (it is now called Lesotho). He went straight to Father Raynes (who earlier had taught him Greek and also he had a great respect for his judgement) to ask his advice as to whether he should accept this Bishopric. Typical of Father Raynes he told Eric to go to the Post Office and send a cable to the Archbishop agreeing to become Bishop of Zululand. Then he said 'we will discuss it!'

Father Raynes knew Eric's qualities and knew he was perhaps the only man who could put Zululand again on the map. Eric agreed to be Bishop if Father Raynes would agree to become Chairman of the Association in England. Father Raynes agreed and said he would try and find a suitable secretary to run it. He found me and for better or worse I did the job for 27 years until I retired in 1977.

I must describe this remarkable man Father Raynes. He had no small talk. His conversation was always on subjects that mattered. He had only one aim in life and that was to serve his God as best he could and he certainly did that. He always thought things out before giving an opinion and if the answer was unpopular he gave it just the same. He was completely honest. He was a person you either hated or loved. You could get on with him or you couldn't. I loved him dearly and got on so well with him although at first I was rather afraid of him. Miles said this was because of his great holiness which shone out not only in his appearance but by everything he said. People stood in awe of him.

I remember before Council meetings started we would all be sitting round the Board room table waiting for him to arrive. When he came into the room everyone stopped talking and stood up as a mark of respect. At my first Council meeting which was held in Tufton Street, Westminster, I was very shy and very frightened.

When I stood up to read my report he whispered to me 'sit down'. He always put people at their ease. I was not used to speaking in public anyway much less to speaking in front of Monks, Bishops, Priests and titled people but once I got to know them they were very easy and very kind to me.

My problem was, what was I to do? Here I was seated at my desk in my little room next to my bedroom in Wantage with my typewriter in front of me but not having a clue as to what was expected of me. I knew nothing about Zululand or Swaziland I hardly knew where they were on a map. I had in my mind's eye a picture of a missionary sitting with his bible under a palm tree with lots of black people sitting around in a circle listening to his words. I really knew nothing about the work I was supposed to pass on to others.

First, I wrote to Africa for slides and scripts in order to get a picture of the country and its people but at second hand this was not very satisfactory or convincing. After doing this job for about six months, Father Raynes said at a Council meeting that he thought it would be a good idea to send me to Africa so that I could see for myself what was being done in Zululand and Swaziland.

Frank Doherty

Margie, Sister of Miles & Wife of Frank Doherty

Frank Doherty at Lancing College

Phyllis and Margie

1950,
White Lodge, Wantage

Fr. Raymond Raynes,
C.R. Mirfield

Phyllis

1951, My first car, Ixworth

Miles, Phyllis, Mary at Ixworth Vicarage

Phyllis and Cat

Phyllis in Garden

*Father Raynes said at a Council meeting
that he thought it would be a good idea to send
me to Africa so that I could see for myself what
was being done in Zululand and Swaziland.*

Owing to various reasons, we left Wantage and Miles was appointed to Ixworth Vicarage in Suffolk where we stayed for 6 years. It was on April 23rd, 1952, that I made my first visit to South Africa. I was young and full of energy and the prospect of the adventure was tremendous though I must admit tinged with fear. It is one thing to travel to an unknown country with a companion but to step out all alone is quite another. In addition, I did not know anyone in South Africa and I knew I was expected not just to enjoy the trip but also to assimilate everything I saw so that I could give a vivid picture to the people in England when I returned.

I remember saying my goodbyes at Ixworth Vicarage and really not saying them at all because I was close to tears at leaving both my sister and Miles. However, once I was on my own I was all right. I remember Miles saying that he would try to write sometimes and I knew then he was feeling as emotional as I was. I took the train to London and stayed overnight with friends who, the next morning, came to Waterloo station to wave me goodbye as I left for Southampton. I met some girls on the boat train so by the time I got to Southampton I did not feel alone.

How big the ship looked! At last I was on the Union Castle Ship,

The Edinburgh Castle and I hung over the rails as we set out with tugs pulling us and a hooter going full blast. We made slow progress and the band struck up National songs – the *British Grenadiers, Rule Britannia* etc. but when they played *Auld Lang Syne* and England was slipping into the background and the people on the docks were getting smaller and smaller I felt a tightness in my throat. I knew I was on my way to South Africa and would not see England again for six months. I must have been very trusting in those days for it was not long before someone had taken a much valued brooch from the lapel of my coat which I had left in my cabin. After that I was much more careful to look after my luggage. As always if one is travelling to a diocese in South Africa by ship you are asked to take with you, in addition to your personal luggage, things for the mission such as vestments, altar linen, etc. to save postage which even then was expensive.

Therefore, I had a lot of luggage with me, most of which was put in the Baggage Room until I reached my destination. There is a smell, at least I have always thought so, peculiar to all liners and each time I have travelled by sea I recognise the smell immediately I step on board. We took three days to reach Madeira and the weather was rather cold but thankfully the Bay of Biscay calm. I wrote postcards home which could be posted at Madeira and spent my time exploring the ship.

The ship could not harbour at Madeira as the waters were too shallow so we anchored some distance away from the island and had to walk down the gangway and go into the little boats which took us to Funchal the capital of Madeira. I went with a party of four, two girls and two men. By this time the weather was hot and sunny and everything looked quite beautiful. We hired a car and driver and went to the top of the mountain to see the famous monastery. We had a rather erratic Portuguese driver and we travelled around at great speed and at great peril round the hairpin bends.

The inhabitants of the island threw camelias into the car singing out 'for you, for you' until we got to the top of the hill where we visited the Monastery and looked round the lovely island. It was so hilly that all their planting was done very neatly in terraces.

Everyone who visits Madeira and who is reasonably young goes down the mountain side on a wooden sledge. Two of us sat in front and two behind with two Portuguese men holding onto the sledge by ropes attached to it. We went down at an incredible speed and the sparks were all around us from the contact of the sledge with the stoney ground. I did wonder what would have happened if the men holding onto us had let go or fallen but it did not happen and we arrived safely at the bottom, all breathless and laughing rather hysterically after the exciting and hilarious adventure.

In Madeira there were wine merchants to be visited and lace to be seen, but I had very little money and the time to buy would be on my return trip home. Eventually we got back on the ship and little boys appeared from nowhere all round the ship and dived into the sea for pennies which were thrown by passengers on board. This went on until the ship left Madeira for Cape Town.

Now the voyage really began. The weather got hotter and the games were brought out and competitions arranged. I played in all the competitions and got first prize for deck quoits and table tennis. The swimming pool was there for your use at all times and there was sunbathing on deckchairs. Ice creams were brought round in the hot weather instead of coffee and hot drinks. You could buy alcoholic drinks very cheaply once you were out of territorial waters.

I was introduced to Pimms and Tom Collins. These 'sundowners' before dinner in the evening were good times. The meals at first I found terrific and I was staggered by the breakfast, lunch and dinner menus. I was thoroughly greedy and made the most of the delicious food but after a short time when the weather was hot, my appetite faded which was a good thing from the point of view of my none too slender figure by then!

I was in cabin class and we had two settings for meals. I always made for first sittings as I am naturally an early riser. Quite often we would swim before breakfast and do our stint of walking so many times round deck to do our quarter of a mile. The days were spent lying in the sun playing games, talking and playing cards. Canasta was the card game we played. One makes friends easily on board but once you land your fellow passengers go their way and I went mine and these new friends were forgotten.

There was a Chaplain on board so Mass was said once or twice during the week and on Sunday everyone turned up for the morning service with the Captain and crew and we sang lustily *For those in peril on the sea*. Also, there was the Captain's reception or drinks party to which we were all invited. As we crossed the line, there were great festivities and Father Neptune performed the ceremony of crossing the line when we reached the Equator which was great fun.

Also there were pillow fights on a greasy pole across the pool which was fun to watch. Every night there was an entertainment of some kind. Film shows, competitions, dancing etc. I had many conversations with other passengers and I was rather horrified when white South Africans advised me not to talk to Black Africans on board because they told me that white people do not speak to black people on a social level, only to give orders.

Phyllis in London on way to S. Africa

Ship to S. Africa

Judging Fancy Dress Contest

Captain's Party

Phyllis on board ship

Phyllis on ship leaving Southampton

*"I was rather horrified when white South Africans
advised me not to talk to Black Africans on
board because they told me that white people
do not speak to black people on a social level,
only to give orders."*

said I did not agree with this but was only told that
when I get to South Africa I would understand the
situation better. We landed at Cape Town after a
fortnight on board from Madeira and we stayed some four days
there. I was glad to have the opportunity of seeing this beautiful
city. I will never forget arriving and seeing Table Mountain with its
snow-clad white tablecloth and the twelve apostles jutting out
along the coastline.

The sea had receded and much land had been reclaimed. I
enjoyed going down the famous Adelaide Street and visiting
Stutterfords, the big store, seeing the Botanical Gardens and the
Houses of Parliament. I visited friends in Cape Town during the
day and slept on board at night.

We then did the Coastal trip up to Durban travelling by night
and spending the days at Port Elizabeth, East London and then we
landed at Durban. The Bishop was to meet me at Durban and I was
a little nervous and apprehensive because I did not know him. I
remember sitting in front of my mirror in my cabin putting on my
hat (for in those days we wore hats) when suddenly I saw the figure
of the Bishop reflected in the mirror standing behind me. He said
'Are you Miss Sargent?' I said 'Yes'. He then said he was going to call

me Phyllis and said 'Let's get off the ship and find your luggage'.

He was friendly and I liked him immediately. He showed me round Durban and I was fascinated by the Rickshaw boys with all their feathers and gay attire and when they danced all round me the Bishop said if I showed so much interest we would never get away from them. I was fascinated by everything I saw. The monkeys in the road and chattering up the trees, the vast distances, everything seemed to be on a grand scale. I was so enthusiastic that the Bishop said he felt that he was seeing the country afresh through my eyes.

When we motored as far as the Tugela River the Bishop stopped the car and said that here I should take off my shoes and stockings and walk barefoot through the river into Zululand which was the other side. It was a wonderful moment, I was actually in Zululand, the country I had been trying to get a mental picture of since Father Raynes asked me to do the job some years before.

1952, on steps of Bishop's house at Eshowe, Phyllis, Bishop Eric Trapp,
Archdeacon Hoddinott, Edna Trapp

African People

African Child

Zulu Mother and Child

Phyllis with Local Zulus

A Young Zulu

Fr Peter Biyela, Zululand

Phyllis, Fr. Barnabas Simelane

After Mass, African Priest, Phyllis

Swaziland

Bishop Alpheus Zulu

"Because one is black and another
white should there be such a difference
in standards, should one have
everything and the other nothing?"

I visited so many places. Empangeni, Gingindhlovu (two gins and I love you!), KwaMagwaza, Ngutu, Nongoma, Etalaneni, Kambula to mention but a few of the names of these places which were pure magic to the ear. I wanted to meet the African people to see them in their homes, to worship with them in their churches. Because one is black and another white should there be such a difference in standards, should one have everything and the other nothing?

The Zulus are a wonderful race, laughter is never very far away. Those who live in the Reserve areas live as a family unit in beehive shaped huts made of wattle and daub with only an opening for the door. No windows. You will usually find a fire burning in the middle of the hut and the smoke rises upwards through the reed roof, so it is advisable to sit on the floor to avoid the smoke getting into your eyes and everywhere else.

Many huts form their home which is called a Kraal. Parents and small children sleep in one hut, sisters in another and brothers in another. Usually there are relations living with them too and 'Gogo' (Granny) is usually the boss. The huts are arranged in a circle and often there is a hedge all round to keep the cattle from straying or being stolen.

The Zulus were a nomadic people but now they are so overcrowded that there is no place for them to move on to. The best fertile coastal land is occupied by the rich white farmers, the sugar barons. The land the Zulus have is very poor, overgrazed and often not enough grass to feed their cattle.

I will never forget my first stay in the Capital, Eshowe with the Bishop and his wife Edna. The roads were dirt roads and corrugated and if you travelled by car the dust came through the floorboards of the car and there was dust in your ears, eyes, mouth, hair and everywhere. When a car passed you it took some time for the dust to settle again to enable you to see the road ahead.

Walking into the little town of Eshowe you would meet Zulu men and women and they would call out to you 'Sabona' which literally means 'I see you'. It is a greeting and I in turn would reply 'Sabona'. They were always laughing it seemed and talking loudly and continuously.

I will not forget the first African church I went to – I did not really know what to expect, but I had not conceived the poverty I would find. The churches were mostly made of mud with corrugated iron roofs, usually painted red. Inside it was very hot in summer for there were very small windows and the floor was smeared with cow dung. There were very few furnishings, an improvised altar with altar linen discarded from our more affluent churches in England. Flowers were in jam jars, no pews but perhaps some benches but most people sat on the floor. They crowded in, men sitting one side of the aisle and women on the other. Children were in front, mothers and babies and young people next and old people at the back. There would be no organ or piano but the Zulus love singing and they harmonise naturally and are not a bit self-conscious.

One of my loveliest memories is of sitting at the back of one of their churches way out in the Reserve and listening to the Zulus singing in their fascinating language with all the various clicks. This singing can always bring tears to my eyes. I remember going to a chuch, when I was staying at KwaMagwaza, in one of the outstations and when we were returning home in the Archdeacon's car we gave a lift to some little boys who were in charge of the collection. I must add that quite often the collection was in kind, for instance instead of currency, it might be grain or chickens and one had to ensure that part of the collection did not eat the other!

Years later I was speaking of this to our second African Bishop and he said that he was one of the little boys in the back of the Archdeacon's car! Later that same young Zulu took a degree in Selwyn College, Cambridge and got a distinction in Greek and he is now the second black bishop of Zululand – Lawrence Zulu.

All Zulu people live below the poverty line but their generosity knows no bounds and after a Service in church they will entertain you royally. I remember after one Service that I went to, one of the women of the Kraal came up to us and said that they were very poor and could only afford to give us a crust of bread and a cup of tea.

We thanked her very much and said that would be lovely but after we were given a cup of tea, a feast was brought to us of chicken with all the trimmings. The Zulus love to give surprises but I felt we were eating food they could not afford to have themselves.

Another time when we were eating chicken at a Kraal, the African priest took a spoon and scooped out an unlaid egg from inside the chicken, which I understand is a great delicacy but I'm afraid I refused to eat it. However the priest, Father Barnabas Similane ate it with great relish as well as a cup full of grease! I learned the next day that he was not feeling too well! Flies are everywhere and the Africans just let them crawl all over their faces without seeming to be bothered by them. It was instilled in me that water must be boiled before drinking.

The Zulus drink from the streams and water holes where they wash their clothes and themselves. No wonder the water is polluted if you have to share it with your cattle and your other household chores.

I said earlier that cattle are very important to the Zulus as it represents their wealth. If you have many cows, you can have many wives for a young Zulu man has to buy his wife with so many head of cattle. So when a girl becomes of marriageable age, the parents fatten her up as Zulu men like their women to be fat. When I first went out to Zululand and the Zulu women walked all around me and then said 'Young lady, you are nice and fat!' meaning I should be married.

"What a country of contrasts is Africa. Some have everything and others nothing. Is it right that if you happen to have a white skin you have all the privileges and if a black skin, none?"

I though the saddest plight of the African was that all able bodied young men must go to the towns to get work for there is no work for them to do in the Reserves where they live. These young men usually go to Johannesburg to work in the gold mines or the other big towns or harbours where they can find work. They go to Johannesburg for six months at a time and then they come home for a few weeks and then back again to the mines for another six months and this is the pattern for the whole of their working lives.

They are not allowed to take their wives and families with them, they have to stay in the Reserve and so often the Reserve is full of young women and children, old women and old men. How can a man be faithful to his wife when he has to live apart from her for most of their lives.

Of course so often the young man in the town finds another woman and forgets all about his first wife in the Reserve. She has to exist with no money for often she cannot trace her husband. I found this migratory labour one of the biggest problems and causes of unhappiness.

The Government insisted on its policy of 'Apartheid' the segregation of black and white people. The white man usually lived in a beautiful house with everything he could desire – money, swimming pool, tennis court and servants while the Africans lived on the edge of cities in a black area where they were crowded together with very poor housing and sanitation.

The Government then started to remove Africans from the Reserve areas to live in African townships. The Zulus did not decide where to live, that was decided by the Government. Often they had no work to go to and were taken away from their friends. There were so many injustices in South Africa. People were held without trial, put under house arrest. Police could raid and search African homes without a permit and this often happened at the dead of night. Children were roused from their sleep, terrified, and perhaps one of the members of the family would be taken away.

Sometimes Africans were banished to Robben Island and often nothing was heard of them after they went there. Also there was one set of rules for the white people and another for the Black. Black and White people could not marry. However black and Coloured people could marry and in that case they would have to live in a Black area and not a Coloured area.

The Coloured people are those of mixed marriages and this started first when South Africa was colonised by the Dutch and the English and others in the 17th century. The Dutch Reformed Church, the Church of the Government, the Nationalists, who originally were the Boers from Holland, justified themselves about Apartheid. They said that in the Old Testament it says that Black people were born to be hewers of wood and drawers of water. However, the Roman Catholic and Anglican Church and other denominations maintain that this is quite wrong and that

"God made all people in His own image and
we are all one in the sight of God."

In our Church, there was no Apartheid. Services which were held in separate churches were for varying reasons. There was the language problem and also geographically it was not possible for all to worship together. However, everyone was free to worship in any church at any time.

I was interested to find outside Cape Town Cathedral a large notice saying that all persons may worship in this church, whatever their colour, at any time. This was signed by Tom Savage, Dean of Cape Town Cathedral who later became Bishop of Zululand.

Africans love an occasion and after a Service, if there is a visitor, there will be speeches. I had to speak through interpreters. Then there would be present giving and then the meal. The Zulus are very sociable and very generous and love things to last a long time. The longer it takes the more important they think it is. Time is not an important factor and often when one is asked out at a certain time, you may ask if it is Zulu time or our time!

When I stayed at a Mission House right out in the Reserve miles away from any town, the first thing I would find out on arrival was what the plumbing was like. Usually non-existent and the 'little house' as they call it would be some distance away from the Mission House for obvious reasons, say 300 or 400 yards or more. My host on once occasion told me that if a white flag is lodged in the door it would mean that someone was in there. If no flag was flying then you could walk up to the little house and fix a flag in the door while you were inside. This ensured that you did not have a useless journey. A stout stick was also to be found in the little house for killing snakes. The open trenches attracted the flies and the smell in the very hot weather was very strong and I'm sure very unhygienic.

While I was staying at an all male establishment at Usuthu, I was asked if I would like a bath and I said I would. However, when I was shown the bathroom I found that several doors opened onto the bathroom and none of them had locks. I then turned on the water but found that the water did not flow from the taps, so I was rather relieved that I could not have a bath after all.

I visited an area which was being prepared to receive Black people and without a Pass you could not go. Father Bill, with whom I went, did not have a Pass but he thought it looked very quiet and so we looked round. Suddenly a man appeared from nowhere and Bill said that I was from England and we were looking round. The man asked us to his house and then disappeared. Bill was sure he was telephoning the Police and so we waited for a Police van to arrive. Later he returned with his wife and some tea for us!

On another occasion I went into a Black area with an African priest and he said Mass in a tent. I had not realised that I should not have been in a Black area and as a result of this the Priest, Isaac Dhlamini was sent to prison. I did not know of this at the time but years later I was told this on another visit.

How I loved the African evenings with the hum of insects and looking at the stars so different from ours in the Northern Hemisphere. The Bishop used to point out to me from the Stoep, the Southern Cross.

I remember lying in my bed in my Rondarvel about 150 yards away from the Mission House at Kambula and hearing the beat of tom-toms and the chatter and laughter of Zulus after a wedding. These celebrations often went on all night. I remember too my horror when staying at St. Augustine's, I discovered large hairy spiders all round the walls of my Rondarvel. I made my way back to the Mission House with the aid of a torch and told them of my plight. However, the only comment I received was how lucky I was to have spiders in my Rondarvel because they would eat all the other insects. I returned to bed rather forlornly, blew out the candle and pulled the sheet over my head and slept soundly until morning.

On this first visit to South Africa there was no electric light in most of the Mission Houses. One night I noticed in my bedroom at Gingindhlovu, noises after I got to bed. I got my torch and tapped on my hostess's bedroom (which was on the Stoep, as I was sleeping in her bedroom). When I told Hilda, she merely replied that I was hearing the bats above the ceiling – she assured me they couldn't get into the room. When I was staying at KwaMagwaza I remember there was netting all round the top of the walls in my bedroom and I could see rats running round all night – this I really hated!

When I was staying at the famous hospital at Nqutu in 1952, I slept in a small room on the Stoep which was the room where usually my host and hostess had their breakfast, Drs. Anthony and Margaret Barker. I remember there was no fastening on the door so it did not shut properly and I was exposed to people walking down the road beside the hospital.

There was no electric light and when I woke in the early morning to noises in my room I could not find my torch and my heart was thumping when suddenly something jumped onto my bed. This time I found a box of matches and lit the candle and found to my great joy that my companion was no other than a cat!

All the time I was in Zululand I was very conscious of the Apartheid laws, the 'don'ts' which seemed to abound all the time for the African. They could not live where they wished, they could not stay with friends unless they received permission and a Pass. They had to carry a pass everywhere they went.

Their house may be searched at any time by the Police. They could not go to a cinema unless it was for black people, nor could they bathe on a beach or sit on a bench in a park or drink a cup of tea or coffee in a café unless reserved for black people.

They could not speak on a social basis to white people (though this did not apply in the Church). So life was very unfair and Africans had so little and were expected to work for the white man for very small wages yet with none of the privileges of the white man.

I visited schools, most of them were church buildings which served a dual purpose. Several classes were taught in one room and the noise was unbelievable – how they ever learnt anything will always remain a mystery to me. The African teacher would come out of the school to talk to me but the children carried on working quietly. It is a privilege to go to school and they thirst for knowledge.

When I crossed the border from Zululand into Swaziland which was then a British Protectorate, but now has gained its Independence, I felt I could breathe freely because here there were no laws of Apartheid, where one always had the feeling of being watched.

I returned to Suffolk in September of 1952. On the way home the ship called at Las Palmas where we spent some time before finishing off our journey to Southampton. I will never forget the utter pleasure I felt in being back in England again where everything was so green and lush and the trees seemed to abound everywhere whereas in Africa I was there in the dry season and everything was burnt up and barren. I could not go to Africa in the wet season because I would have been bogged down on the dirt roads.

Village life went on happily and it was lovely seeing all my friends again. One day when I was away at meetings in London the Bishop of St. Edmunsbury and Ipswich and a priest called to see me to ask if I would consider working part-time at the Diocesan office as Secretary to Canon Snell who was Director of Religious Education in the Diocese and about to become the first Residentiary Canon of the Cathedral of St. Edmundsbury. This I did and was very happy in the work which I combined with my part-time work with Zululand.

It entailed all the adult education courses at Leiston Abbey and Youth Conferences at which I used to hostess, organising Bishop's exams for schools and the Annual County Harvest Festival which took place in the Cathedral. Almost at the same time I was asked by the Bishop of Dunwich (the Suffragan Biship of the Diocese) if I would do his letters in my spare time – these I did at home and the Bishop was a frequent visitor to our house.

This was a very pleasant time because I did three days a week in Ipswich and had the rest of the week for Zululand – also I had all the energy I needed in those days and life was fun. The only snag was Miles' health – he suffered from a bad heart and had many coronary thrombosis attacks which frightened my sister and me as we thought on many occasions that he had died. Often he had a heart attack while taking a service in Church or just going upstairs one evening when he could not be moved for many hours. After that particular attack we brought his bedroom downstairs and he was in bed for six weeks.

While we were at Ixworth Vicarage our house was usually filled with people and it was quite usual for seven or eight people to appear in our kitchen for elevenses!

I must mention, a short time before I left Ixworth for South Africa I was asleep in my bed and was awakened by the sound of taffeta passing down the corridor outside my room. I always kept my door open in case Miles was not feeling well and called out. I looked towards the door and saw a shrouded figure gliding down towards my sister's bedroom at the end of the corridor. I told Miles about this next morning and he said not to tell Mary before I left for South Africa.

Strange to tell the following year at the same time I saw the apparition again and saw it was making its way down the corridor towards my sister's bedroom. My sister came into my bedroom early next morning and greeted me with the words 'Phyl, I had an apparition in my bedroom last night and the cat's fur stood up straight in fright'. I replied 'yes, I know, I saw it making for your room'.

After six years at Ixworth, the Bishop asked Miles if he would be his Chaplain and go to a very small village about two Miles from Bury St. Edmunds where he could take retreats and Schools of Prayer at which he was so good and also to look after the small parish of Fornham All Saints. So in October 1956 we moved house once again.

1956, Fornham All Saints Rectory

1959, Fornham All Saints Rectory, Miles and Bishop

Miles, Phyllis, Mary at Fornham Rectory

*O*ur new home was very lovely, part Tudor and part Georgian with a large garden surrounded with lovely trees, chestnuts with pink flowers, lilacs, laburnums among many others. We made good friends in Fornham and enjoyed our short stay there very much.

On December 18, 1958 our beloved Miles died. He had not been well and a week before Christmas all the carol singers were invited into the Rectory for hot soup and refreshments. I remember going to bed that night and going to Miles' room before going to bed to ask if he was all right. I knew he wasn't but he hated us to fuss.

Luckily Mary heard him in the night and we telephoned for our dear friend and doctor, Michael Mackenzie, who stayed with Miles until he died. This was at about 4am and I remember Mary and I did not go to bed, we went down to the Church and pinned a notice on the door to say there would be no communion service that morning as the Rector had died.

One old lady came to the door later with tears running down her face. She could hardly speak but thrust a currant cake she had made into our hands and said that it was 'something to go at'. Later we gave her Miles' watch. Jim who lived next door to us gave us £5 for ourselves in memory of Miles as he did not believe in buying flowers. A Priest from a nearby town came to see us and he said with tears in his eyes 'Remember that God never makes mistakes'.

At these times it is the kindness of ones friends that stands out and God seems to give one the knowledge of his presence and because everything is in God's hands it is all right. This peace lasted for some time, I suppose until the initial shock was over. I will not forget the kindness of the Bishop who came to see us the night Miles died. He had driven over from Ipswich and was taking a Retreat for Ordinands at the time. He told us he had to come. He said he loved Miles and that Miles was one of the first friends he made in Suffolk.

1958 was a memorable year for me because in June my beloved Chairman, Father Raymond Raynes also died. The Bishop of Zululand and Swaziland left Zululand to take up an important post in England as Secretary of the Society for the Propagation of the Gospel (now USPG, United Society for the Propagation of the Gospel). This meant that he was in charge of all missionary endeavours for the Anglican Communion in the world.

Canon Snell for whom I worked in Ipswich was made Archdeacon of Bedford and later St. Albans. When he left Suffolk my contact with him ended. After Miles died we had three months to move out of the Rectory. Everything in my life had literally changed overnight.

I remember this time most vividly and it was strange that through it all there was a sense of calm and no panic. This was in spite of the fact that my jobs had changed through people leaving and my home had been broken up and those I loved most had died or left the area. In addition to this Miles' sister had died the week before Miles' death and he had asked me to go to the funeral in Sussex as he did not feel well enough to go. We little thought the following week he would also be dead.

Bishop Eric Trapp was replaced in Zululand by Tom Savage who was at the time Dean of Cape Town. This was because it was Lambeth Year, which is held every ten years when all Bishops from the Anglican Communion assemble in London from all parts of the world.

Tom Savage, now Bishop of Zululand came to England for the conference and I had to arrange a deputation tour for him to meet supporters of the Zululand Swaziland Association in England. At the same time, the new Bishop had to appoint a new Chairman for the Zululand Swaziland Association in place of Father Raynes who had died. He chose Father Michael Westropp, one of his closest friends. Michael had worked with Tom Savage in South Africa some years earlier and was Godfather to his son, another Michael.

I remember so well my first meeting with Michael Westropp. Bishop Savage invited me to lunch at Church House, Westminster and Michael was to be there also. I even remember I was wearing a blue lawn dress and a hat. I remember very little about the lunch but I do remember saying goodbye to the Bishop and Michael in Tufton Street and Michael said to me 'We will meet again'. That was the beginning of a very long friendship which continued for many years.

When I returned to the Rectory in the evening, Miles asked me what I thought of the new Chairman. 'Pompous and top drawer' was my reply! At that time I was still grieving over the death of Father Raymond Raynes and felt that no-one could ever take his place.

However, Michael has been a wonderful friend to me and still is. I suppose I have shared most of my sorrows and hurts with him. He was a wonderful Chairman, very energetic and expected me to have the same drive as he had. I think he usually got what he wanted out of me for I too was full of energy and enthusiasm for doing all I could to raise money and interest people in the two dioceses I worked for. Through Bishop Trapp's dedicated work he re-established the diocese once again on the map. When Bishop

Savage took over the reins it was a going concern but more funds were needed and my new Chairman's first aim was to send out more money from England to the diocese.

This meant that I would have to travel the length and breadth of England calling on parishes and speaking to all kinds of parish gatherings to raise this extra support. Michael promised the Bishop that we would increase our giving by £500 each year for the next five years and this by hook or by crook we did.

Up till then I had done barely any public speaking and basically I am a very shy person with little confidence myself but gradually I got used to it and was encouraged by the wonderful people I met all over the country. I remember talking to a parish in London in my early days. I confessed to the Vicar at Supper that I felt nervous. He told me not to think at all about myself or my feelings but just to remember that my audience loved me. This I found a great help because people are and were so nice and kind and helpful. Therefore, I suppose, it was really my pride which made me nervous because I wanted my talk to be a success.

It was suggested at a Council meeting that we should produce a Christmas card to sell for the Zululand Swaziland Association. I asked through our magazine *The Net* for ideas and as a result of this a Mrs Margot Tyrie wrote to me and suggested we lunch together. I met her at Wormwood Scrubs prison, where her husband Derek was Chaplain.

Margot was able to help me with the Christmas card because she knew all about that kind of thing and was Director of a large Book Shop in Brighton. She was also the original organiser of 'Feed the Minds' which is now run in a professional way and very much to the fore in helping the Third World obtain books.

Margot and I became great friends and I spoke to the prisoners at the Scrubs which was a great experience. After my talk I met the prisoners and Derek told me that three men who were speaking to me at one time were all in for murder. One of these chaps sent me Christmas Cards for many years and I rather wondered whether he would appear on my doorstep after his release, but no, happily he met someone and they got married.

I remember the Chaplain telling me amusing stories, for example, the time the Bishop was coming to celebrate Mass in the Prison. Derek and a prisoner were serving the Bishop and afterwards the prisoner said to Derek 'How nice to have three Cambridge men in the Sanctuary'. He also spoke of an actor who was in for a short term and afterwards invited Derek to a party on his boat on the Thames. Derek and Margot went to the party where there were many celebrities from the acting world and these people kept saying to Derek who was wearing his cassock 'How on earth did you meet…'? Derek could not say where they met for obvious reasons.

At home, life was continuing as usual but after Canon Snell left Suffolk I continued working in Ipswich for a short time. I eventually gave it up and became a part-time secretary to the new Provost of St. Edmundsbury Cathedral. Miles Chaplained the Bishop at the Provost's installation and that was his last public engagement, for Miles died the following week.

I was working hard for the Zululand Swaziland Association and also for the Provost and I found doing two part-time jobs too demanding. Doctor MacKenzie said I would have to go slower. It was then that I was feeling rather low and depressed as I was missing Miles more than I thought possible. I did not know the new Bishop of Zululand as I knew the previous one and I was missing Father Raynes and did not know the new Chairman very well either.

So after the next council meeting in London, I asked the Chairman if I could have a word with him after the meeting. I told him how I felt about the Zululand Swaziland Association and how I felt that it would be better to get a new secretary in my place as all the key people I had known had been replaced (Father Raynes, Bishop Trapp, Miles). Miles had edited the magazine *The Net*. Father Westropp said he thought I had better sit down and proceeded to tell me that he thought I should on no account think of resigning but considered it necessary that I did the job full-time. This I did, and it was a great relief to make the Zululand Swaziland Association my full time work as I could not do justice to either job and my health was suffering as a result of it.

It was in March 1959 that my sister and I bought a rather nice Georgian town house in Bury St. Edmunds for £4,500. We then moved into it on Friday 13th March, 1959. Without Miles' stipend we found it very difficult to make ends meet as we had no widows pension. My sister and I had very little money of our own because most of what we had went into the buying of the house. We then had all the upkeep of the house and food etc. My salary was not enough, so we took in paying guests.

This was not a very happy arrangement but we did have one or two very nice people who stayed in our house. On the other hand, we had some very undesirable ones. The house was on three levels and later on we made the top storey into a flat consisting of a bedroom, sitting room, kitchen and bathroom.

We had no separate entrance so we all used the same front door. It was most unpleasant having people in and out of our house at all hours, especially in the early hours of the morning. However, there was no alternative if we wanted to keep body and soul together. We had to share our home with others.

We have always had animals and we brought two cats, Nicholas and James with us from the Rectory and they settled into town cats very well. We had a tree, lilacs and laburnums and lots of hollyhocks, irises and beautiful roses and a lawn. We stayed and managed in this house somehow or other for fourteen years.

Life was very busy at that time with the Zululand Swaziland Association and as well as attending our own meetings in London, I was on the USPG African Sub-Committee and the South African Church Institute which were held every six weeks or so in Westminster. It was lovely attending the United Society for the

Propagation of the Gospel (USPG) meetings for my first Bishop of Zululand, Eric Trapp, was now Secretary of USPG and he chaired all the meetings. I remember one morning at a meeting, he wrote a note and handed it to me over the Boardroom table and it said 'I have just become a Grandfather – will you have lunch with me'? I used on most occasions to have lunch with him after the meetings which I thoroughly enjoyed.

I often met priests before they went to work in Africa and I remember going to the home of a young priest in Chelsea to tell him about Swaziland before he sailed. When I arrived at his beautiful home in Old Church Street I was met by his mother, who was probably one of the most beautiful looking women I have ever seen. She was probably in her sixties when I first met her but she was quite beautiful in appearance as well as personality. She was anxious because her son was ill in bed with flu when I arrived and had a high temperature and she did not think him fit to travel to South Africa the following day. I went to the shipping company and arranged for her son not to have to queue anywhere but to go straight aboard ship where he could go to bed at once in his cabin. Lady Salmon never forgot this and we were close friends from then on.

On another occasion I remember having lunch with a young priest shortly before he left England for South Africa. He was single, 29 years old and had all the makings of a good priest, full of enthusiasm for work in the Diocese of Swaziland where he was going. I remember so well that lunch in Westminster for he told me that he had been to school at Radley. Once when found by one of the Masters in a place where he should not have been, he quickly thought of his excuse which was that he had been looking at the Notice Board for he had seen a Course to which he would like to go.

This was all made up on the spur of the moment for he had no interest at all, he told me, in the course which was being held at Lichfield, on the training of Ordinands. However, he had let himself in for it and when he got to Lichfield he was so impressed by all he heard from Miles Sargent who was doing the Course, that he there and then found a vocation to the Priesthood. He then had no idea that Miles was my cousin and I marvelled at the way God works.

First Miles implicated in getting Peter interested in the Priesthood and now here I was talking to him before he set out for South Africa. Some years later I saw him in Swaziland and he took me round to the various mission stations and when we arrived back at Usuthu for a late lunch all there was left for us to eat was a plate of black sausages covered in flies!

During the twenty seven years I worked for the Zululand Swaziland Association I made three visits to South Africa. First in 1952 when Eric Trapp was Bishop, then in 1962 when Tom Savage was Bishop and lastly in 1970 when Alphaeus Zulu was Bishop of Zululand and Anthony Hunter Bishop of Swaziland. I travelled mostly by sea but in 1962 I flew to South Africa.

I flew from London airport to Luxembourg and then the plane developed engine trouble and we had to spend the night in Luxembourg. The next day we did not manage to fly but were taken on a trip by bus into Germany and when we got back to the hotel found the flight was still not on and later in the evening we had to get a train and go to Brussels.

We finally left Brussels Airport at 2am. By this time I was past caring what happened. We then flew for twelve hours to Lagos in Nigeria where we landed for re-fuelling and then flew for another twelve hours right across Africa to Lorenzo Marques, Portuguese East Africa. We arrived there at 4am and were put up at a hotel as there were no connections at that hour of the morning and the priest who had come up from Swaziland to meet me by car had to return as it was Saturday and he had to be back for the Sunday Services.

The priest left a message with the Missions to Seaman Chaplain, who looked me up and looked after me during the day. I was collected the next morning by Father Anthony Molesworth and taken to Piggs Peak in Swaziland where I was due to stay for two or three days. This was the pattern of my stays in Africa. I was handed on from one mission station to another and spent two or three days at each place.

I thoroughly enjoyed all my trips and especially the visits to the Game Reserves. I will never forget my visit to the Hluluhuwe Game Reserve. I went on my first visit in 1952 with Denis Rutt, who later became a Canon of Lichfield Cathedral. The Game Reserve was part of his parish. We toured round before going to the Centre and it began to get dark (as there is no twilight in Zululand) and he couldn't find the way. He had to put on his lights, although one is not supposed to put lights on. Eventually we found our base and I was very glad to get into my Rondarvel which would be my home for the night.

Denis took me to see the Warden of the Game Reserve and we had drinks with him. He told us all kinds of stories about the animals and how rhinos had appeared in his garden and how the tick birds eat the ticks off the animals backs and how the zebra is always near the Wildebeest as they are said to protect the timid zebras. When we got back to the base for the night there was a terrible thunderstorm and it was really frightening. I half wanted to find Denis but was afraid to leave my Rondarvel. I learnt in the morning that he did not like the storm either.

The next day we had a guide called Hamilton and he took us on a tour of the Reserve which was fascinating. My last visit to a Game Reserve was in 1970 and I went in a party with Bill Hardwick, rector of Mtubatuba, Zululand and a married couple. Bill loved the Game Reserve and had no fear at all and his wife said to me before we left, 'don't let Bill get you out of the car for the animals are wild.' But not so, we left the car and were amongst forty rhinos. Bill said that if they pound their feet on the ground or put their heads down, take off your shoes and run for the car.

We saw a lot of animals and the deer were so lovely to watch.

The Kudo, Impala and wart hogs were so funny and I am sure they have a strong sense of humour for often we had to wait while they crossed the track where we were approaching. They followed one behind the other with their tails erect.

My return journey in 1962 was by boat and I was staying at the Bishop's house just before I was due to leave for Cape Town. However, I developed a temperature and fainted at mass. I stayed in bed and the doctor gave me an antibiotic and said I would be well enough to travel in three days when I was due to leave Eshowe.

As my time drew near to leave Eshowe, I knew the antibiotics were not working but I said I felt fit because I did not want to inconvenience the Bishop by staying in his busy house any longer. Father Anthony Salmon motored me down to Durban and put me on the train for Cape Town. He did not like leaving me for he knew I was unwell but I said I would be all right. The Bishop made me promise not to board the ship if I did not feel fit.

The train journey took a day and a half and I laid on the couchette with my clothes on and with my temperature rising to over 104 degrees. I felt sure that I wouldn't reach Cape Town alive as I felt so ill. I tried to say the Lord's prayer but could not get through it. When we finally arrived in Cape Town, I didn't know how I was going to manage with my eleven pieces of luggage and feeling so ill. I managed to get a porter and asked him to take me to the Settler's Club (that is where the Bishop told me to go) and when I arrived there I could hardly speak. I asked for Miss Dix and told her I was ill and would she put me up.

Miss Dix knew the Bishop, as he was previously Dean of Cape Town Cathedral. She said 'My poor child, you are ill, take her up to Number 36.' I was taken to room 36 and all my luggage was brought up with me. I had an en-suite bathroom and blissfully had a bath and then got into bed. At that point I did not care what happened because at last I could relax. Miss Dix was wonderful. She got a doctor to see me and he came twice a day for a bit. The doctor said I had pneumonia and pleurisy and that I had to stay in bed for a fortnight and then another fornight to get fit.

After that point I could travel home on the *Windsor Castle*. As I was not insured for illness I had no money to pay for the hotel or the doctor so I asked Miss Dix if she would kindly cable the Bishop and ask him if he would lend me £50 until I got home when I would repay him. The cable came back with the words that the money was coming and I was to accept it as a gift. When I finally arrived back in England I only had a three penny piece left in my purse!

I have had strange experiences when doing deputation work around the country. I have been greeted on the doorstep by my hostess at a vicarage where I was due to speak that evening, with the words 'Ham or Spam?"

I have stayed in many strange beds but one of the most scary ones was after I had done a talk in Buckinghamshire and was driving onto Cookham to stay the night with my Chairman and his wife. Just before I reached Aylesbury a terrible fog descended and I had no idea if I was on the right or left hand side of the road. I was afraid to stop because of traffic bumping into me and I had simply no idea where I was as I was dependent upon signposts which I couldn't see.

I did stop however, when I was sure I was by the kerb and everything was uncannily quiet and then I heard footsteps coming in my direction. I put my head out of the car window and asked if I was on the right road for High Wycombe. A female voice said 'you will never get there tonight dear.' I asked where I could put my car for the night so that I could walk into Aylesbury and find a bed for the night. She then told me to put my car in a siding nearby and added 'you can stay in my cottage if you like. It is simple but clean.'

I thanked her and telephoned my chairman from a phonebox nearby to say I was staying here for the night. I did add that I was feeling a little apprehensive about my night's lodging. My Chairman's reply was "oh the Holy Spirit will look after you – see you tomorrow." I did not feel so confident!

Later, as I sat by the fire in her tiny sitting room watching the loud ticking clock behind me reflected in the window opposite, my hostess said she could see a figure behind me. She added that she was a psychic and would like me to go to a Séance with her which I declined. Later she took me up to my bedroom and told me that the sheets were aired because she had slept on them, they were under her mattress! The bed was very high and I almost needed a ladder to get onto it but once I was there I sank into the middle of the feather bed. She came into my room a little later and asked if I minded whether she said goodnight to her Guardian and Guide. She then proceeded to make overtures to the two pictures hanging on the wall, one an aesthetic looking nun and the other a turbaned Indian gentleman. After she left the room I slept soundly until morning. In the morning, I had a cup of tea, thanked her and gave her something for my night's lodging and made my way to Cookham to stay with my Chairman.

The grandest house I stayed in was when I was invited to speak to a Parish in Devon. I spent the weekend with Mr. Denis Rhodes and the Hon. Mrs Rhodes. Denis was a member of the the Zululand Swaziland Association Council. I am not likely to forget that weekend as Margaret Rhodes was a cousin of the Queen, the daughter of Lord Alphinstone. I was very nervous at the prospect of staying with them, but I need not have been because as I drove up the long drive and arrived at the large, imposing house, I was met by Mrs Rhodes who greeted me with the words 'you must be dying for a cuppa.'

Their kindness, understanding and courtesy was tremendous. After a short time Mrs Rhodes asked me to call her by her Christian name, Margaret. In the course of the conversation she said that it was by accident of birth that her Aunt happened to marry the King of England (George V1). I was very impressed by the beautiful house and the lovely things in it and was fascinated by the photographs of the Royal Family in her drawing room.

We had drinks before dinner and then wine flowed freely at the dinner table. We then had coffee afterwards and socialised into the evening. It was an insight to see how the other half lived. There was a television programme on one evening that they were anxious to watch,'Till death us do part'. They probably thought of me as a bit churchy and that I might not approve as sometimes the language in that programme was perhaps a bit borderline. When I said it was a favourite programme of mine also we all watched it together and thoroughly enjoyed it. I had to open a fete on the Saturday afternoon and speak on Sunday morning.

Another grand house I visited was the home of Lord Plunkett in Kent and here again I knew Pam Plunkett who helped me with 'Health and Welfare Covenants'. We had an excellent lunch and I met Pam's husband, Kiwa, who was most charming and related to Denis Rhodes. My chief recollection of the house was the bathroom and lavatory where the walls were covered by autographed photographs of prominent film stars.

I met Denis Rhodes' sister, Maureen Balfour, a very delightful person and also a member of the Council. She also lived in Kent at Birling Place and I visited her at her home and was very impressed by her beautiful rural home where it was hard to imagine it was only twenty miles from Hyde Park Corner.

In 1967 Bishop Tom Savage died from a long and distressing illness and Bishop Alphaeus Zulu was elected Bishop of Zululand in his place. He made history because he was the first African to become a Bishop in South Africa. He had already been a Suffragan Bishop of St. John's Diocese but now he would have his own Diocese of Zululand. At the same time Swaziland had gained its Independence and appointed its first Bishop, Anthony Hunter who was from Huddersfield Parish church in England. So from now on, I had two separate Dioceses to deal with instead of one.

I was nervous about my first meeting with Alphaeus Zulu as I had heard so much about him through the papers and the meetings he had attended for the World Council of Churches in Geneva and other places. In 1968 he came to England for the Lambeth Conference and I had to arrange a tour in England for him to meet his supporters in the Parishes up and down the country.

He was staying in Norfolk with friends of his, Claude and Elizabeth Rutter. They were driving him down as far as Attleborough, Norfolk. I was to meet them there and bring the Bishop back to Bury St. Edmunds. I can remember arriving at the church where we arranged to meet and wondering what he would be like. When the car arrived the Bishop got out, came up to me, shook my hand and called me by my Christian name. I liked him immediately. He was shorter than I had anticipated but with such a warm personality, so vital, so loving, so direct and his voice and laughter so deep and infectious.

As we drove home in my little Mini Minor car, I asked if he would like me to call him 'My Lord' or just 'Bishop'. He said with such simplicity, 'I would like you to call me Alpheus'. This I must add was in 1968 and we were not so free with Christian names as we are today. His stay with us was a wonderful experience and it was good to find out what it was like to be black in South Africa from an African's point of view.

I remember on another occasion when I was to meet the Bishop from Ipswich Station. I was very excited because I was meeting him on his arrival from Africa. I said to a porter nearby 'I am going to meet off this train one of the most wonderful people in the world'. He looked at me and said 'Are you Miss'. Later after the train arrived and the station was deserted I was still on the platform with my arms entwined round the Bishop's neck with tears running down my face and saying 'Oh Alpheus I am so pleased to see you'. He replied with his lovely deep African voice 'I know, I know'. I then saw the porter looking in our direction and I wondered what he thought but could not care for I was too happy and content.

Previous Bishops of Zululand had of course lived in a white area but as Alpheus was black he could not live in the previous

Bishop's house. So although he was Bishop of white, black and coloured people in Zululand, he had to live in a black area. This wonderful man had more intelligence than most people and he was certainly far more holy and for him to be degraded in this way was heartbreaking for me.

When I visited him at his home in Eshowe for dinner the first evening I arrived in Zululand, we travelled by car through the tarred street of Eshowe and then turned off onto a dirt road which was full of pot holes and had no street lighting. We bumped along with dust everywhere until we came to his house in the black area of Eshowe. Once inside his house there was friendliness, joy and love. We had a wonderful meal cooked by his coloured wife Miriam in a happy contented atmosphere.

I must add that I could only visit the Bishop, I could not stay the night in his house because I am white and he is black. What a strange world we live in. It is so stupid that there should ever be a colour bar although segregation is not a colour bar but a cultural one and it operates in every society whatever the colour of your skin.

In May 1969 I had a letter from the Archbishop of Cape Town, Robert Selby-Taylor saying that the Province wished to honour me with the Order of Simon of Cyrene which is an honour given to lay people for work done in South Africa. Only fifty people can have this honour so when someone dies the Archbishop nominates someone to make the number up to fifty. I was both delighted and humbled when I had this letter and Bishop Zulu said he was coming to England in August and would invest me in the Cathedral of St. Edmundsbury. This was arranged and friends came from far and near and the Provost of St. Edmundsbury offered me his house for the reception after the Service.

This was and is one of the highlights of my life and I will never forget that service or the Bishop fastening the Order of Simon of Cyrene round my neck on a blue ribbon and saying 'Phyllis I invest you…' It was a very moving moment and one that is sacred to me.

August 26th 1969 was a wet day but nothing could dampen my spirits. In the morning bouquets of flowers and telegrams arrived at the house which made me feel more like a bride to be than a middle aged spinster!

Many friends arrived from afar and I had arranged for some of them to be put up at friends' houses in the town. At lunch time, Anthony Salmon arrived (a priest from Zululand) and took me and Bishop Zulu to the Angel Hotel for lunch.

The cathedral filled up in the evening for the Service and it had been tastefully decorated with flowers, as had the Provost's house for the reception. The Service was recorded and I often listen to the recording just to reassure myself that it really happened.

36 Churchgate Street,
Phyllis and Mary, leaving for Church

Eric Trapp, Bishop of Zululand and Swaziland

(from left) Provost John Waddington, Tom Savage Bishop of Zululand and Swaziland (after Eric Trapp), Precentor of St Edmundsbury Cathedral, Phyllis

St Albans Abbey, Bishop Alpheus Zulu, Phyllis, Bishop Eric Trapp

1961, Michael Westropp, Chairman ZSA

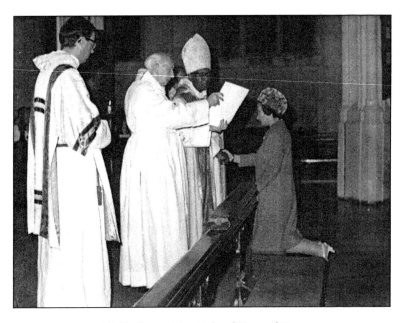

1969, Phyllis receiving Order of Simon of Cyrene

*Phyllis at Open-Air Mass at KwaNzimela celebrating the
Centenary of the Diocese*

Mary in Rose Garden, 36 Churchgate St, Bury St. Edmunds

4 Crown Street

4 Crown Street, Drawing Room

Bishop Alpheus Zulu, Phyllis at Dr Barker's flat in Wimbledon

William Sanders, Bishop Alpheus Zulu, Phyllis
at Dr Barker's flat in Wimbledon

"In May 1969 I had a letter from the Archbishop of Cape Town, Robert Selby-Taylor saying that the Province wished to honour me with the Order of Simon of Cyrene which is an honour given to lay people for work done in South Africa."

*T*he Reception was held at the Provost's house and a beautiful feast had been organised. I wore the Order around my neck and felt very humbled by the whole thing. Bishop Zulu stood on the stairs in the middle of the large hall and people gathered all around him while he talked to us. It was then that he said I must visit Zululand once again. This I did for the Centenary celebrations in the following year, 1970.

In 1970 I paid my last visit to the Diocese of Zululand and Swaziland and it was a very memorable one because of the Centennial. An open air Mass was sung at KwaNzimela where a large Altar had been erected and a huge cross dominated the scene.

I was included in the huge procession of clergy wearing the Order of Simon of Cyrene. During the Service I sat close to the Altar just behind the Zulu Royal Family. About 9,000 people had converged on KwaNzimela that morning for the Service and it was a joy to see Black, White and Coloured people all mixed together. No segregation on this occasion and as I looked across the vast arena it reminded me of the Feeding of the 5,000 in the Gospel.

It was a beautiful day with a clear blue sky and everyone was joyous and happy in this Celebration of a hundred years of blessing. It was very moving to watch all the thousands of people surging forward towards the Altar to make their Communion. Priests who were Administering the Sacrament to Black, White and Coloured people all coming up in any order without any segregation whatsoever.

After the Service we had a sumptuous feast in the open air and the meeting together of so many friends from all over the two dioceses and beyond. Many Africans had made a special effort to be at this Service and had come many miles. They travelled by car, bus, bicycle and some on foot, in many cases taking days to arrive at KwaNzimela in time for the Service. It was a memorable time for me because I met many people I might not have met but for the Centenary and the spirit of happiness and thankfulness pervaded the whole day.

I will never get used to picking oranges and bananas straight from the tree and having an avocado tree in the grounds of the hospital at Kwamagwaza. What a joy the fruit was and how good it tasted.

During this visit to Zululand I was taken into an African Township early one morning and collected in the evening. It did not occur to me at the time that I would be one white person among all those Africans but they were so welcoming and there was such a deep love among these people that anxiety did not enter my mind.

Looking back on it now I wonder at the marvel of being given this privilege of sharing one day with these people. We had a Mass in the morning and then I met a lot of the Congregation. Photographs were taken and this was followed by a wonderful meal which was produced by some of the women. How we all crowded into that little house I will never know. It seems that whether a church or a room is full, there is always room for more people to crowd in.

In the afternoon I was given a tour of the Township. We went through dirt roads where children were playing in the streets. Their toys were rough carts they had made themselves. The houses were very poor, no more than shacks with corrugated iron roofs with little or no sanitation. Several houses shared a lavatory in the yard. I was taken to a shop where I bought some sweets for the children. However, the store keeper would not allow me to pay for them.

I saw the bus which took men to their work and I was interested to see there were huts reserved for the single men to sleep not in the township but away from it. The huts were floodlit all night to prevent night visitors, although the Township itself had no street lighting. I enjoyed my day very much and felt that I understood these people just a little more after spending a day with them. I could appreciate their problems and frustrations after seeing their way of life.

Chief Gatsha Buthelezi who is Prime Minister of KwZulu (Black Zululand) and related to Bishop Alpheus Zulu and the Royal Family of Zululand invited me to have lunch with him when I was staying near his home. Gatsha is a very intelligent man and has a degree. He is spokesman for the Zulu people. Sometimes the Africans feel betrayed by him because he has many white friends and they think he perhaps makes too many white friends. However, this is unfair for he is completely honest and works wholeheartedly for the black man and is dedicated to the betterment of the African people. He is a practising Christian and has been to England many times.

It was a great honour to be invited to his home and there I met several people including his mother, The Princess Magogo and his wife, Irene. Before lunch we had a drink and nuts and other snacks were passed around. We had this in his large hall.

Chief Gatsha Buthelezi explained that the lunch would be a very simple one, however when we moved into the dining room I found a long table and many guests seated. The table was laden with all kinds of delicious foods. The Chief laughed when he saw my surprise.

He sat at the head of the table with his mother at the opposite end. His wife served and did not sit at table. I sat on his right. It was all most beautifully done and a most enjoyable meal. He was an excellent host, though rather a shy person. He laughed a lot which I felt was a reflection of his nervousness.

After lunch we went again into the hall and his mother, the Princes Magogo, played for us on her ugubu bow. This was a great honour because Chief Gatsha told me that he did not think she would play for us. Gatsha sang along in accompaniment. She played a love song she has composed in memory of her late husband and then a joyful song of the Resurrection. I was given presents by the Chief before I left. This was a great experience and I felt it was a very great honour to have been asked to visit him in his home. Shortly afterwards I returned to England.

In the summer of 1973, we were just going to have lunch when someone rang the doorbell and I found a young man on the doorstep. He wanted to know if we were interested in selling our home. I said 'not at the moment, but when I retire in a few years time we will have to sell it and buy a cheaper one'.

He explained that his firm wanted our house more than any other property in Bury St. Edmunds because they owned the Georgian house next door and our house would complete the block as it was bordered on each side by a road. He also said that if we would sell him our house they would give us a higher price than anyone else. He asked where we wished to live and I told him that I would like to stay in this area. He said that his firm owned a property across the road and if we liked it we could come to some agreement.

Later in the day I telephoned my chairman, Michael Westropp and he told me not to do anything about the house until he had come to Bury. He and his wife Rachel drove down from the Lake District the following day to see the house. When we looked over it we all felt 'this is a must'.

So in December 1973, we moved across the road to 4 Crown Street with no regrets. One of the Canons of the Cathedral, Jack Churchill, told us that this was our Heaven sent house and it proved to be exactly that. How good is the Lord, how well He provides for us!

Bishop Trapp said to me some years earlier that he did not know how we would manage financially when my time for retirement came but he added that God would work something out because you cannot work all your life for the Church and not be provided for in some way. He certainly did and this house has been and still is such a Blessing and its Peace has been noticed by many who visit us.

Possibly because this house was part of the old Abbey and it still retains some of the atmosphere. I am told we were part of the Mint, but we have found no trace of it. We moved into 4 Crown Street on December 15th, 1973 along with all the builders, electricians, plumbers and painters.

We had the walls painted from coloured to white and we had to have the roof repaired and the central heating system revised. However, once these alterations were complete it was the perfect house. We have a small walled garden which leads to the Cathedral churchyard and opposite across the green are the Abbey ruins, the original West front of the Benedictine Monastery which I believe was the largest in Europe.

My sister and I moved to this house with my little King Charles spaniel, Emma. Our two cats had departed this life but it was not long before we acquired another black and white stray cat with the largest eyes and white whiskers imaginable. He had been chased up a tree in the churchyard and couldn't get down. When eventually he was coaxed down by Canon Cecil Rhodes and Dr Dick Gaman, I brought him in and gave him some food. I remember Canon Rhodes saying 'I somehow don't think you have seen the last of him!' Of course he was absolutely right, he made his home with us and we called him 'Magnificat'.

I remember the time of our move very vividly because of two things. In particular, a week after we moved into the house I heard that a very dear friend had died and I mourned his death very much indeed. It was a private grief because not many people knew how I felt about this death.

The other reason for remembering the move into this house was that after some months of living here I was awakened every morning at about 3 a.m. with the sounds of beautiful singing. I got up and looked out of the window onto the churchyard but could not see any signs of where it came from. This went on for a long time and when I spoke to the deputy organist at the Cathedral he merely said,

"What you are hearing is the monks singing
their offices – of 500 years ago!"

I since learnt that there was another person living in the churchyard who also heard this singing and she said it was exactly like the Plainsong she had heard in Notre Dame in Paris. When they were excavating the ruins the singing was continuous. I have not heard of anyone else who heard it and most people were sceptical. However, I know that it was not my imagination. One morning after I had heard the singing I said out loud 'the whole world is full of your glory'.

After working for Zululand and Swaziland for twenty seven years I knew the time to retire was not when you could no longer do the work entrusted to you. I decided to retire on 6th February 1977 when I was sixty. I would lay down this wonderful job with all the marvellous people I had met both in South Africa and throughout the length and breadth of England.

I remember so well my last council meeting which was held in St. Edwards House, Tufton Street, London, the House of the Cowley Fathers. I was very tearful because I could hardly bear to think that this was my last meeting, the last time I would meet these

Council members who had become so dear to me.

Michael said to our host, Father Naters, Society of St. John the Evangelist (Cowley Fathers), 'When you speak to Phyllis do not mention her retirement', but Father Naters came up to me and I told him I was feeling very sad because this was my last meeting with the Zululand Swaziland Association. He helped me by suggesting that I went with him to see his roof garden. I did this and found it very beautiful and strange to see this colourful garden on the roof top of this beautiful house overlooking Westminster Abbey.

In June 1977 at the Annual Festival held in London, I was given a Presentation – a beautiful brooch of garnet and pearls and a cheque for £500. I was very touched because Bishop Trapp made the presentation and was most kind in the things he said about me and then six Council members got up and also spoke. This I found very moving especially when the whole meeting sang 'For she's a jolly good fellow'. This proved too much for me and although I wanted to thank everyone, especially those who had travelled long distances to be there, I sat down with tears collecting in my eyes. My sister, a friend and my King Charles spaniel, Emma, came to London with me so fortunately I did not have to travel home alone.

Giving up this job was like a little death to me and because I never married, it had filled my whole life. I could not think how I would exist without the Zululand Swaziland Association. How was I to fill my life? A new secretary was appointed in my place and I handed over to him all my office equipment and projector and this was the final parting with my job and my life as I knew it.

The greatest hurt was losing contact with the many friends I had made through the job over so many years. I cannot describe the hurt that went on inside me because I felt I had lost all that was dear to me.

For a year and six months I rested for I was very tired but it did not take me long to realise that retirement was not for me because it was plain to see that I could not live on my small income. I had received a car allowance so was not sure how I could keep my little car.

It happened that I was invited to a drinks party over the Christmas season to some Architects who lived nearby. I did not know them particularly well but my host asked how I was enjoying my retirement. I told him that I would have to look for a part-time job that was not too demanding on my advancing years. He said that if he heard of anything he would mention my name. I thanked him and the next day he telephoned to say that he knew of someone who needed a part-time secretary and for me to telephone the person. I did so and was engaged in this capacity to a firm of Quantity Surveyors in Bury St. Edmunds, Lewis and Marshall.

The work was varied and I answered the telephone, typed, made photocopies, prepared the invoices and of course made tea! How fortunate I was to have this job because at that age one was thought of as being unemployable. My employer was kind and helpful and it was wonderful being able to earn a little money in this pleasant and happy environment.

I have two cousins who found vocations to be nuns at the Community of the Holy Name, an Anglican Order in Malvern. Mary Alison often spent part of her 'Rest' with me and my sister and of course has been a wonderful help to us spiritually. It was while she was staying with us that she asked if we would go with her to Hengrave Hall to a Charismatic prayer group. My sister and I were terrified at the thought of it but said we would take her there and fetch her after the meeting but that we would not go to the meeting itself.

It was here that our cousin met Father Emmanuel Sullivan, who was the chaplain at the Ecumenical Centre at Hengrave. Father Emmanuel was a Roman Catholic Franciscan monk. The Prayer Group was an Ecumenical one consisting of about six people. Mary and I were interested but very shy and would not say prayers out loud.

It was on another occasion again when Mary Alison was staying with us that she asked us to go to a Charismatic Healing Service which was held in a church nearby. I was not well at the time, in fact I had been running a temperature for some time and had an appalling cold, so we asked a friend to drive us. The four of us went in the car along with my dog, Emma, who was so tiny she could sit on my lap without being noticed.

It was one of those rather rowdy affairs with lots of singing of choruses and clapping of hands. Mary Alison told us afterwards that she was so afraid that all the noise might put us off forever, but we were quite impressed in spite of it. Mary and I did not do much as we were too inhibited. At home my sister, Mary Alison and a friend laid hands on me with prayer. I knew that I would be alright. That night, my cold just disappeared and from that moment on my temperature was normal. I knew it was the result of their laying hands on me.

Later I made a Retreat at Hemingford Grey, which was conducted by Father Humphrey Whistler CR (a monk from the Community of the Resurrection at Mirfield). I learnt much about praying from him and that Retreat brought me in touch with Rosemary Carr who has since proved to be such a good Christian friend.

One day when I was driving up alone to London to a Zululand meeting I was praying and thought that I might have been speaking in tongues. Some time later a friend and I were having coffee with two people in a nearby village. I did not know them very well but they were interested in prayer groups and while we were there we talked about praying. One of them put their hands on my head and immediately

"I seemed to be in a black box, then grey and then suddenly it was as if the lid had burst open and everything was white and bright. I could not help

speaking in tongues and at the same time tears
were running down my face and I was filled with
such joy and warmth."

This was my first experience of speaking in tongues but I am aware that many people are sceptical about this. I can only say it is one of the gifts of the Spirit, if only one of the lesser ones, but to me it was wonderful because it came as a proof that God loved ME and I was a person in my own right. He had given this gift to me and that alone was a revelation and something I can never forget and will always be thankful for. Of course speaking in tongues is a Heavenly language and when we don't know what to ask God for or how to pray, or if we just want to praise God, we let God speak through us and of course when one is tired and praying is difficult, speaking in tongues is a help.

"At our prayer meetings sometimes the whole
meeting will sing in tongues and it is quite
beautiful and the sounds harmonise and often
when one person speaks in tongues sometimes
someone else in the group is able to interpret it."

It was when we got to know Rosemary Carr that we decided to go over to Hengrave each Friday evening to pray with the Ecumenical Prayer Group. By then the group had grown and often there were 25 people there or even more. It was a very powerful group.

Afterwards we had coffee in Father Emmanuel's house and I remember speaking to a very nice American woman called Marie. I told her that I did not think this kind of praying was for me. She turned to me and said that that was the Devil speaking to me and went on to say that it was no good coming one week and then not again for two weeks but that I should come every week for 3 months and if I still found it was of no help then I must stop coming. I took her advice and my sister and I plodded along every Friday for 3 months.

Before long we felt compelled to go each week. In those early days I sat very quietly and never uttered a word but was just carried along by the rest of the group until Father Emmanuel said one evening that we all had to contribute. I somehow knew he was speaking directly to me and the next week I made myself say something. I felt dreadful and my voice sounded cracked but I had done it and from then onwards it became easier.

On another occasion Father Emmanuel thought we should not just be a cosy group and so we prayed and asked the Holy Spirit what was required of us. Father Emmanuel said we should wait until our prayer was answered. About a quarter of an hour later a young girl of about 16 years said that she thought she ought to start a Prayer Group in her school which she did and which has continued through the years.

It seemed to be required of us to start another Prayer Group in Bury St. Edmunds and so Rosemary, Mary and I started this new Prayer Group in our house which we held every Monday at 8pm. This proved a great success and grew in numbers and from then onwards we had our group on Mondays but we still went to Hengrave on Friday evenings.

It was later decided to form a core group and six of the prominent people with the most experience of praying and prayer groups were asked to form this group. It consisted of about six people including Father Emmanuel, two or three nuns and the rest lay people, one of whom was Andrew a very dear friend to us all. This core group met regularly and made plans for the Prayer Group and took turns in leading it each week.

It was at this time that we met Andrew who had joined the Community at Hengrave. He was an Anglican in his early sixties but his growth as a Christian, one could almost visibly see. He had tremendous problems in his life in spite of being a wartime pilot with all the courage and bravery that entailed and he was a very able engineer and a good administrator. Sometimes he would telephone us and ask if we were going to be alone that evening and if so he would like to come and see us.

When he came we would talk about God and on one occasion he told us how difficult he found it to love God the Father as he had not got on with his own Father. In time all that was put right and he had a revelation about his father, an almost physical presence of him and an assurance of his love. He also spoke about the Devil and his experience of a visible Devil and how it sometimes came towards him in the form of a huge toad with a diamond sparkling in its forehead. He told us how terrified he was and he made the Sign of the Cross and told it to go back to Hell. It did not go away but simply melted into nothing. Andrew had a long and painful death but during those last few weeks of his life he was able to put right everything in his life which had not been good.

Each member of his family came to see him from all parts of the world and the wrongs were all put right. When people visited him in hospital they nearly always found him praising God. I never hear or sing the chorus or hymn 'My God how great thou art' without thinking of Andrew and thank God for his witness and for the privilege of having known him.

While at Hengrave the core group ran a 'Life in the Spirit' seminar. This course lasted for seven weeks and was most inspiring. At the fifth week we had the laying on of hands and at the time many people did this course and they had the laying on of hands in the lovely Chapel in Hengrave grounds.

This was a wonderful evening and as we came back from the Chapel into the Community Room where we meet, everyone's face was alight and they were smiling and full of joy. That was one of the most wonderful evenings of my life.

I remember so well one particular Monday evening when we were praying in our house, Father Emmanuel, Andrew, two nuns, several other people, Rosemary and my sister and I.

*"The prayer was very deep and at one stage
Father Emmanuel said 'can anyone feel a Presence
in this room?' One person said that she could see a
light which she had experienced twice in her life
before. She said at first she thought the centre light
in the room was switched on but when she opened
her eyes there was no centre light and the light was
still there. At that point she knew there was a
Presence in the room. Emmanuel said 'I know
Jesus is in this room and he is saying I am your
teacher and I will lead you to heaven'."*

That was a very special evening.

As always happens when you love people they leave and so Emmanuel left Hengrave and also a large number of people from the prayer group left the district. Some returned to the States and so we were left with a small number of people mostly from Bury. We formed a new core group of which I became a member and the venue of the prayer group was discussed and it was decided to have it in Bury St. Edmunds in our house at 4 Crown Street.

We stopped our Monday night prayer group and they merged into the Friday group. We had this prayer group in our house for about two years meeting regularly every Friday evening at 8pm. Often 20 to 25 people crowded into our upstairs sitting room (which we called the Upper Room) and used to be my office. We had many wonderful and happy times in that room. We prayed from 8 to 9.15pm and those who wished to stay for counselling or more prayers did so and the rest came downstairs and drank tea or coffee and chatted, often the last to leave was at about 11pm or later.

The core group no longer met in St. Louis Convent, but in our house at regular intervals. At about this time, my sister, who was never very robust was having a great deal of pain in her back and also very bad pains in her stomach. When the pains got worse we called the doctor and he suspected that she had an infected gall bladder. One evening she was in very grave pain and our doctor called in a specialist who said immediately that he thought she should have an operation. When she got over that attack she went to see the specialist, Mr Barabbas and he said the operation was necessary and he would arrange it with the hospital as an emergency.

Mary had the operation in September 1980 and it was worse than they anticipated for stones were found all over her body and the operation was not easy because her back was so bent that her pelvis had hooked round her ribs making it difficult. She recovered from the operation very well but her back continued to be a trial, so much so that she went to an orthopaedic specialist who said there was nothing that could be done for her. She had a disease called osteoporosis which can attack anyone old or young and it is a progressive disease.

Mary and I were both worried because at night she could not lie down because of the pain and often she would spend the night in a chair which meant neither of us slept and we would make tea at all hours of the night. Every six weeks she would have a bad attack which meant that several bones in her spine had fractured and at these times it was pure agony for her. Gradually they mended and then we had to wait for the next attack and this seemed to be the pattern of her life.

It was sometime in 1981 that one of the nuns, Sister Kathleen, asked if I would go with her to Ipswich when David Watson was speaking during that week. He is an Anglican priest and a great Charismatic. Mary could not go because she could not bear the jolting of the car. When the meeting was over we spoke to David Watson and he asked me why I had come. I told him that I wanted healing for my sister. He asked me her name and what the trouble was and then told me he would pray for Mary that evening.

It is strange how God works for it became very clear to me soon after that I must telephone Dr Michael MacKenzie, a medical consultant at the hospital and a friend of ours. He knew of Mary's troubles and I said I thought the problem was not an orthopaedic one but a medical one. He thought I was right and said he would do anything to help. As a result of all this he put Mary on a new treatment and saw her every three months privately without charging her a penny. How kind and good people are!

For years afterwards Mary did not get fractures and her condition stabilised although she was on painkillers, wore a collar and was in constant pain. There were many prayers said for Mary and for me as well and they were answered, though not in the way we intended for she did not have physical healing. Mary was at first resentful and kept asking questions 'Why should I have this pain? Why should my body get deformed and bent, why can't I do the things I want to do?' I in my turn wondered why must Mary be ill, it curtailed my activities and I was terrified every time she went out alone for fear she would trip on uneven pavements or get run over as she was so bent she could not see traffic approaching.

Happily Mary eventually accepted her pain and disability and had a great peace and tranquillity. I no longer worried about her so much and also felt at peace. We both learned to thank God for our circumstances because it is in our circumstances that God wants us and if we opt out we would no longer be doing God's will. It is only through living as He ordains that we can progress in our spiritual state. We thanked God for all He has done and is doing for us.

In the beginning of 1982 another great tragedy came into our lives. Our neighbour, James, aged 36 who lived across the road died in tragic circumstances. He was young and very rich but was divorced from his alcoholic wife who lived in Malta after the divorce. His mother had come to England from Malta as she was no longer able to look after herself and was at the time living in a very expensive Nursing Home in Bury St. Edmunds where James could visit her daily.

It was in March 1982 that I was telephoned from London by a friend of Claire's (James' ex wife) saying Claire was coming to England the next day and wanted to stay with us. I thought quickly and said that it would not be possible for her to stay with us as my sister was not well. I saw James and told him Claire was coming to England and he said we should not put her up because we knew the condition she might well be in. He added she was more his responsibility than ours and asked me to keep him informed of her movements as he did not wish to see her.

About 10pm Sunday evening Claire telephoned from a hotel in Bury (she had been met by the police on instructions from her friends in London). She was in a very inebriated state and said she wished to collect some possessions from her ex husband's house. At the time we had a friend, Henry, in for the evening and we all considered whether it was a good time to ring James and tell him of Claire's arrival or to wait until the morning. We decided to wait until the morning. We thought there was no point in upsetting him.

However, it was too late in the morning as he had taken an overdose of pills and later I went into his house with the police and found him dead at the bottom of the cellar stairs. This was a tremendous shock and the thought still invades my mind that I ought to have been able to prevent this dreadful tragedy. If only I had got in touch with him on the Sunday evening, all this might have been averted.

His suicide meant endless interviews with the police and then the Inquest where I had to appear as a witness. This was all very upsetting. My sister and I went with a Priest and the curator of Ickworth Park to scatter his ashes. James had been a great admirer of the National Trust and spent much of his time and energy helping them. A tree was planted in the park in his memory.

I will never forget those ashes being scattered for it was a windy day and we had to keep moving away to avoid part of James resting on us. I thought of the words said on Ash Wednesday at the Imposition of Ashes Service:

*'Remember O man that dust thou art
and to dust thou shalt return'.*

I thought of James then and how he had been, a tall, spare young man with lovely hair calling to us as he went about town with his shopping bag waving in the air, calling out his greetings. I thought of the lovely dinner parties he gave and the infinite care he took in choosing the right people for each party. He was such a sensitive young man but how I wished I had known of his loneliness.

Our troubles and sorrows did not end with James for his ex wife Claire was still in Suffolk. We were told not to get in touch with her or have anything to do with her particularly before the Inquest. At first I justified these sentiments by thinking of my sister who was at the time not at all well and I was away in the afternoons at my job. So although I felt I should not get involved with Claire as she was drunk most of the time and also the police were investigating her for any implication in James' death.

However, one Sunday morning when I was at Mass in Hengrave Church, it came to me that I must get in touch with Claire. I saw it was not Christian to turn away from someone who was so obviously in a bad way. That day I telephoned her and asked her to come in for some coffee. I asked her on a Monday morning when I knew friends would be having coffee with us and they were people who had been praying for Claire. She did not come that day, neither did our friends, but they came on Wednesday and so did Claire.

She looked so much older than her 39 years and so wild and unkempt. Her hair had not been brushed but there was still the old sparkle of the Claire we knew and loved. I was later in touch with her trustee, Tim Dufort, who came to see her with her brother Ned and they persuaded Claire to go to the hospital to be dried out. By this time she had been from hotel to hotel and had gone through the £1,240 given to her as a settlement from Tim. I visited Claire regularly when she was in hospital.

One day when I visited her she came to meet me tottering down the ward saying 'hello lovey'. She was very drunk and I could get no sense out of her. I saw the doctor who was on duty, but not in charge, and told him to search Claire's bed and luggage but he said he couldn't do that. They had let her go to town to see her bank manager (or so they thought). She had obviously bought some alcohol.

Next morning I telephoned the doctor in charge and he said that my suspicions were correct for they had discovered in Claire's cubicle, two empty bottles of gin and one of brandy. It was then obvious that she must not leave the hospital premises for any reason. Tim Dufort telephoned me to ask if I had any ideas for Claire in the future for she would have to go on a long term treatment somewhere.

I said I knew of a very good place which was run by nuns of the Community of St. Mary the Virgin Wantage but I was not sure where they operated from but would find out. I did and sent the brochure to Tim who thought the place ideal and that he would drive down from Harpenden to visit Spellthorne St. Mary. He did this and was most impressed by everything he saw there.

The nuns stipulated that they would have to interview Claire before accepting her. First of all we had to get Claire's approval to go there for six months. My sister and I visited Claire and told her about Spellthorne, rather dreading what her reaction would be. However, there was no need to worry because Claire jumped at the idea and said she would love to go. This was arranged and Richard Meyrick, a friend in Bury St. Edmunds, drove her there stopping for a picnic lunch on the way.

Spellthorne stipulated that they would not accept Claire if she arrived for interview under the influence of alcohol. She was accepted into Spellthorne and I had quite a battle to have her driven by hospital ambulance when she was later taken there to stay. After meeting with the hospital secretary he arranged for Claire to be taken to Harpenden at 6am on a Monday morning.

She settled in well at Spellthorne and a few weeks later I went with Richard Meyrick to visit her. She had put on weight and looked so lovely and so much younger. How lovely to see the dear Claire we knew. She was so appreciative of all that had been done for her and when she showed me round the house and then the Chapel, we both thanked God for all that He had done for her. We had a lot of things of hers stored at our house and I took them down for her. She was so happy and said it was like Christmas.

It was around this time that my darling little dog, Emma, died. I was absolutely devastated. She had never been a well dog and was always on medication for fits and at the end her heart gave out. She was so brave and courageous and never left my side. I think I wept and lamented her death for three days and decided there and then that I would never have another dog for the parting is too heartbreaking.

After three weeks I could stand it no longer, there was no little dog to greet me when I opened the door, no little dog to sit on my lap in the evenings or to sleep in my room at night. I was completely lost without my dog. So one morning I asked my sister if she would drive over with me to Woolpit to look at some King Charles Spaniels. When we arrived at the kennels we were surrounded by flirtatious puppies. If I were to buy one I decided it would have to be different from Emma in every way and so I decided to have a dog this time rather than a bitch and a different colour if possible.

As I looked at these delightful puppies I saw one, which was younger than the others and was not joining in the fun but sat shivering all by himself at the far end of the enclosure. I knew at once that he was the little dog I wanted. I bought him there and then. He was only seven weeks old and so tiny that he sat on my lap on the drive home. This was on the 14th November, Prince Charles' birthday and so he was called Charlie.

Charlie proved to be a most beautiful dog and although I was told that dogs are not as affectionate as bitches, no dog could have been more loving than Charlie. He was always by my side, so good tempered and so loving. He did all the things that Emma did including coming to church on weekdays and behaving himself as if he understood the meaning of it all.

I thanked God for our animals. Mary had her beautiful black and white cat, Magnificat, who talked to her and followed her around and I had Charlie to make our home complete. All was happy and life went on smoothly.

The only fly in the ointment was Mary's health which did not improve and I hated to watch her in constant pain and discomfort. My life was not as I had envisaged at the start. I imagined that I would be living a life of ease with enough money to cope with our needs but God does not always plan our lives as we would wish and whatever happens in the future He will provide all that is necessary for us.

"I thanked God for all the people who helped me in finding the true life which I so often rebel against but know in my heart I would have no other."

I thanked God for our prayer groups on Monday and Friday evenings and I thanked God for my Christian friends for without them I would not have been able to cope. I find there is always a way out and there are always people willing to help when things get desperate. I thanked God for Father Emmanuel who directed me over all those years and who steered me through the difficult passages and explained how God is working through my life and of this I am confident and grateful.

I would like to say a word about the Church and how it saddens me that we are so divided. This was brought home to me very much when Father Emmanuel had been staying with us and he asked us to go to the Convent with him where he was saying Mass. He said he was so sorry that we could not make our Communion but for the sake of the community this would not do.

So at the time of the Consecration he came down individually to Mary and me and said that we had really received our Lord and he kissed us and then all the nuns in turn did the same. The tears were falling down our faces. This was the first time we had felt the division of our churches.

Sister Kathleen told us that she felt the same as we did about it but it was not until some months later that Sister Kathleen, Rosemary Carr and I were in one of the villages and a priest (an Anglican) wanted Sister Kathleen to have Holy Communion. Kathleen was upset but knew she could not receive the Sacrament from Anglican hands. Again we all felt so sad. Kathleen was crying and so were we and it was then that she understood how we had felt at the convent some months before. This brought us all much closer together and we sang all the way home and were happy because we knew we were all one in Christ.

I wonder what our Lord would do if He came to earth and saw how the various churches treat one another? But of course:

> *"If He came to earth there would be*
> *no communions and no sacraments because*
> *He is the Living Bread and the Way,*
> *The Truth and the Life"*

and then our lives would be complete but this is what we are waiting for and striving after. *

---

* Phyllis' 1977 text seems to conclude at this point in 1984. The rest of the text seems to have been written in 2005 to 2006. It begins with the year 1985, when Phyllis realizing that she had not long to live decided to complete this account with a short resume of her reception into the catholic church.

Phyllis' Reception into the Catholic Church

*O*have written earlier that Mary and I went to Father Emmanuel Sullivan's Charismatic Prayer Group at Hengrave Hall. Father Emmanuel, a Roman Catholic Franciscan monk was Chaplain to the nuns at Hengrave. It was a large Prayer Group consisting mostly of Catholics and a few Anglicans and others. We met every week for an hour of prayer and then had coffee and refreshments in Father Emmanuel's house. After a time we got to know him pretty well. He was a very learned man of great holiness who agreed to help me spiritually and for several years guided me and gave purpose and direction to my life.

Recently I have received a letter from Father Emmanuel which contains his recollections of this time:

I met Phyllis when I arrived to help establish what we came to refer to as the 'Hengrave Community'. While we were planning the formation of this community and running down the girls school associated with it, I was free to discover new friends in the course of sharing in prayer groups. As time went on, the prayer group grew until we had to find a special room in the grounds of Hengrave. It was a remarkable development and grace for all of us. Two very refined ladies, Mary and Phyllis Sargent, became regular members of the prayer group. Phyllis always brought her little dog named Emma who was carefully kept under her splendid mantle. Since Emma was well behaved and well out of sight and not interested in prayer she would fall asleep beneath Phyllis's mantle and snore away. I knew this was not a member of the group and failed to associate the snoring with anyone. Eventually I found out that the source of the snoring was coming from beneath the mantle of Phyllis. Thus I came to meet Emma and enjoy the company of Phyllis and Mary. What follows proves that God does work in mysterious ways His wonders to perform. Mary and Phyllis in time opened their home and hearts to our prayer group and our friendship within the group produced this wonderful bond of friendship between Phyllis and myself. Her friendship with me has been so open and solid that it has become very much a constant in my life.

Our meetings were happy and easy in spite of our differences of religion. Mary and I had been unhappy in the Anglican Church for some time and my sister was far from well.

We could not get to our usual church so worshipped at the Cathedral which was almost next door to us. It wasn't quite what we wanted, in fact we were both very unhappy and we didn't know where to turn for help.

By this time Father Emmanuel had been recalled to his Mother House in America. Before he left he told me that he thought the priest who could help me was Father Dermot Fenlon but I did not know him and he was a Roman Catholic. I did not think he would entertain having close contact with me, an Anglican.

It was in the year 1985 that a friend from the Prayer Group asked us if we would invite the same Father Dermot Fenlon for coffee. He had not long come to St. Edmunds Roman Catholic church as curate. He had held important posts in Cambridge. He had been a Fellow and Tutor in History at Caius College and had lectured in the University of Cambridge, so he was a late seminarian.

Father Dermot came to Bury St. Edmunds in his early forties after being at the Beda* in Rome for four years training to be a priest. Mary and I secretly thought it was rather pointless to meet with him to discuss our faith as we were Anglicans but anyway agreed. Father Fenlon came for coffee the following Tuesday.

The morning proved to be very rewarding and we asked him to supper the following Saturday. He came and we agreed to meet each Saturday if we were free to do so. When he arrived about 6pm we said an Office and then had supper. After supper we talked about the Catholic faith. Mary and I asked endless questions and Father Dermot had great patience with us and talked to us with great simplicity. These evenings were pure magic and the hours flew by. We both looked forward each Saturday evening to his visits. It was these meetings with Father Fenlon that gave us our sanity, hope and faith for the future.

All this time Mary was ill and could do less and less for herself. She was in great pain, bones in her spine fractured every six weeks. Then a pain specialist came and gave her an injection and she was better for perhaps another six weeks but these fractures came round regularly and the pain was terrible, so bad that many nights we did not sleep at all. Mary was very bent and I had to do everything for her. This was not easy for me either because I was doing a part time secretarial job as we did not have enough money to live on after I returned from my African job. Also I had to look after the home and do all the chores and bathe Mary every night. So each day was mapped out. Mary was becoming worse and I was

---

* The Pontifical College in Rome named after St. Bede, was established in the 19th Century for Anglican converts and later vocations to the Priesthood among Catholics.

getting to the stage where I felt I could not carry on much longer but there was no other way.

It was about this time at one of our Saturday evenings that we asked Father Dermot whether we should change our religion and become Roman Catholic. Father Dermot had put no pressure on us but we could see he was pleased and I think perhaps he thought it was the right decision. He left no time in setting things in motion and we were to be received into the Roman Catholic Church on February 27th, 1987.

It was the beginning of 1987 that Father Dermot told us that he would be leaving Bury St. Edmunds to go to Norwich Cathedral for a few months before going to Oscott where he would instruct seminarians into the Priesthood. Mary and I were devastated to hear of this change and felt life was going to be too difficult if Father Dermot was to be taken from us.

He told us that a Father John Drury just got back from a five year stint in Peru and was to be our parish priest. I remember our saying 'We don't want Father Drury, we want you', but Father Dermot said we were very lucky to have him. Just before Father Dermot left Bury he asked Father John Drury to come and meet us.

At my first meeting with Father John he came to tea and asked Mary and me why we wanted to come into the Catholic Church. Mary and I warmed to him at once as everyone does. He had a quite magnetic personality and lovely large brown eyes. Everyone loved him, he really was quite exceptional, so full of fun and so good and holy also. We were indeed lucky to have him for our parish priest. However it didn't dim our sadness in losing Father Dermot.

When the date came near for our being received into the Catholic Church, Mary was ready so I suggested to Father Dermot that Mary went forward and I would follow later when I felt sure. Having worked for the Anglican Church for 27 years in my Africa job, there was a strong feeling of disloyalty. I had received many letters mostly saying I was letting down the church which had supported and nurtured me and I felt guilt and unhappiness in what I was proposing to do.

Father Dermot said we could both wait until I was ready and then we would be received into the Roman Catholic Church together.

When Father Dermot left Bury St. Edmunds he said he would come on his way over to Norwich to have coffee with us. It was late January and very cold with snow on the ground. I felt so sad that I cried for three weeks after he left Bury. I walked over the road where he had parked his car to say my goodbyes. Mary could not walk so she said her goodbyes in the house.

In early February 1987 we had friends in to celebrate my 70th birthday and that evening when I let my little dog Charlie in from the garden I fell and broke my arm and leg. I could not move and lay on the hall floor. Mary somehow got to the phone and an ambulance arrived to take me to West Suffolk Hospital. We arranged for someone to come and stay with Mary while I was away. Father Dermot came to see me from Norwich whenever he could and I did see Father John occasionally.

I had the accident four days before we were due to be received into the Catholic Church. *

However, I was received into the Catholic Church by Father Dermot from my hospital bed three days after my operation. Mary was received in our home on the same day. All so different from what we had anticipated. Two nuns, Sister Kathleen and Sister Anna were our sponsors and they came to West Suffolk Hospital for me and then to our house for Mary.

---

* This seems to indicate that Phyllis had arrived at a clear decision after a period of deliberation. What happened next was an accident which seemed to necessitate her immediate reception into the church. Given her age and frailty Father Dermot's decision was made on the basis of what seemed like necessity.

Phyllis and her cousin, Sister Mary Alison

Fr. Emmanuel Sullivan

Fr. John Drury

Phyllis, Mary and Cousins

*1988,
Peter Burtwell,
Mary, Phyllis,
Charlie*

Phyllis's sister Mary at 4 Crown Street

Mary's Last Years

*O*ver the next few years, Mary's health did not improve, in fact she could do very little for herself. It was on Christmas Eve 1989, when Mary and I were saying our prayers that I suggested we ask God to do something for us. We knew we could not go on like this much longer. Mary really unable to do anything and I was so tired that I knew I could not carry on much longer. We loved each other but the pressure was too much.

Christmas morning 1989, Mary was taken to St. Edmunds church in a wheelchair by Peregrine Hubbard (who had been so good to her). I couldn't go because I was not fit enough. She was radiant and was wheeled to the front of the church under the Christmas tree and kept saying afterwards 'I made my communion on Christmas morning'. Father John told me afterwards that she looked just like the Queen Mum!

The next morning when I was getting the breakfast I heard Mary call and at that moment our nice helper came in and went straight up to Mary's room where she discovered that Mary had fallen on the floor. Mary could not move or speak. The doctor arrived and our kind neighbour, Elizabeth from across the road went to the hospital with Mary in the ambulance. I was still on crutches so waited at home.

After the ambulance taking Mary left the house someone knocked on the door. It was a friend I hadn't seen for a long time, Jill Carsen. She said, 'are you alright? I had to come.' When she found out about Mary she stayed with me for the night. How good is God!

Mary had had a major stroke and was in a coma for 5 days. She died in the early hours of January 1st 1990. Those days were so sad. I was taken to the hospital to see her, then wheeled to her little room. I held her hand and spoke to her of how much I loved her. I said 'if you know I am here squeeze my hand' She did this for two days but after that there was no response. I knew she had gone. I remember so clearly, people I recognized from St. Edmunds, kneeling and praying in Mary's room. They were members of the St. Vincent de Paul group and when I came to see Mary they disappeared to leave us in peace – such lovely people.

Sister Kathleen came to see me and I asked her to try and get me in touch with Father Dermot. He was in Ireland at the time but eventually she tracked him down and he said he would telephone me a bit later which he did. I remember little of the funeral as I was quite numb. Father Drury and Father Dermot took the funeral service and they came to the house afterwards along with many friends and relatives who have been so good to me over the years.

March 2006

Conclusion

Ilove my home and dear little terraced garden. I still drove my little Renault car until last year which enabled me to get to St. Edmunds Church every day to make my communion. After my dear friend, Father Dermot left Suffolk he finally ended up in Birmingham as an Oratorian where he is so happy and fulfilled. Although removed from Suffolk he still keeps in touch with me and has helped me immensely over the years.

I also used to drive into Essex each week to see my cousin but now this is not possible due to my failing health and the fact that I am now registered blind. I have many good and lovely friends who keep me in touch and help me in so many ways and my next door neighbour turns up from time to time with a bottle of champagne.

I could mention many dear friends in Bury St. Edmunds but they know who they are and I won't mention them all by name in case I miss out someone who has been good to me. Also my cousins in Essex keep in touch by telephone and with occasional visits. I am filled with gratitude for all of my many friends who have helped me throughout my life.

Looking back on nearly 90 years of life I have so much to be grateful for. I realise too that I have missed out on so much. I would have dearly loved to have a special person to share my life – a husband, children but that was not to be. I think my life has been enriched by so many wonderful people and experiences. I would never have had if I had been married.

"I have never had wealth, in fact very little money, but inherited the love of devoted parents and brother and sister. We knew the love of parents and had a very happy childhood. I think we all received their love of God."

I spend a lot of time alone now and I have the Statue of Our Lady in my drawing room. She looks after me and guards the house and God is always my constant companion. He lives in me and he is my strength and with him I converse all the time. I find it easy to make my confession regularly now as I am approaching death and find the Sacrament I receive gives me so much help and grace.

"Death is a friend but of course I fear it because it is something one has to do alone but I trust completely in the love and mercy of God. When the time comes I will be ready."

2007, Phyllis at her 90th Birthday Party

Think of Me

BY JOAN HIGGINS

'Think of me,' she said.

'Oh, my dear, goodbye,' she said
And gave to me her farewell kiss of peace,
Remembering the past that's fled,
The heart's possessions slowly shed
As in this present blinding dark,
    eternal lights increase,
'Please, think of me,' she said.

Each time the sun arises in the East
    then travels west,
Awaking all to share the feast
Of Christ, as longed for guest.
Then think of me, your friend,
And lift your heart to God in sweet request
    to lead me to a holy end.
'Oh, yes, my dear, remember me,' she said.

Phyllis's goodbye to Arlene*
September 21st, 2006

---

* Arlene Rowden was an early member of the Hengrave Prayer Group where she
first met Phyllis.